CHEMICAL EXAMINATION

OF

ALCOHOLIC LIQUORS.

BY THE SAME AUTHOR.

12mo, cloth. $1.75.

OUTLINES

OF

PROXIMATE ORGANIC ANALYSIS.

FOR

THE IDENTIFICATION, SEPARATION,

AND QUANTITATIVE DETERMINATION

OF THE MORE

COMMONLY OCCURRING ORGANIC COMPOUNDS.

CHEMICAL EXAMINATION

OF

ALCOHOLIC LIQUORS.

A MANUAL OF

THE CONSTITUENTS OF THE DISTILLED SPIRITS AND FERMENTED LIQUORS OF COMMERCE, AND THEIR QUALITATIVE AND QUANTITATIVE DETERMINATION.

BY

ALBERT B. PRESCOTT, M. D.,

PROFESSOR OF ORGANIC AND APPLIED CHEMISTRY IN THE UNIVERSITY OF MICHIGAN

NEW YORK:
D. VAN NOSTRAND, PUBLISHER,
23 MURRAY STREET, AND 27 WARREN STREET.
1875.

NEWBURGH STEREOTYPE CO.

PREFACE.

THE numerous inquiries from chemists for some guide or for references to use in proving alcoholic liquors, and the steadily increasing demand, in the author's own experience, for a manual to diminish the task of personally directing students in this branch of commercial analysis, have led to the preparation of this little work—as a help to the analyst. It has been shaped by the design, firstly and as a necessary basis for analysis, to place in outline the chemistry of alcoholic liquors, including their current impurities and adulterations, in such terms as to be understood by persons having only an ordinary acquaintance with chemical science. Secondly, to furnish directions, so far as possible, for an efficient chemical examination, not more elaborate than required for commercial, hygienic, and legal purposes, and containing all details except such as are found in the first books of chemical analysis.

With no desire to fix the comparative importance of the prevalent impurities in alcoholic liquors, the writer, in common with very many persons, holds it to be of absolute importance to society that all articles used as foods, medicines, or beverages, be made subject to strict scientific examination by authority of the law, and that concealed impurities and additions be systematically exposed and suppressed. Legal provisions to this end, now being rigidly enforced in all other countries with which this consents to be classed, are nowhere more necessary than in the enterprising, inventive, instable, and eager commerce of America, and here at last and at a time not distant, they must be initiated. For that time let analysts be prepared.

The author acknowledges his great indebtedness, not only in this volume, but as an analyst and teacher, to the authorities and collators to whom he has given references, and to others whose contributions have been so long published and so well established as to render personal reference unnecessary.

University of Michigan,
Ann Arbor, December 17, 1874.

CONTENTS.

PRODUCTS OF THE ALCOHOLIC FERMENTATION AND ITS ACCOMPANYING CHANGES.

CONSTITUENTS OF THE ALCOHOLIC SPIRITS AND LIQUORS OF COMMERCE.

THE CHEMICAL EXAMINATION OF ALCOHOLIC LIQUORS.

TABLE OF REFERENCES: AN OUTLINE OF THE ORDER OF EXAMINATIONS.

CHEMICAL EXAMINATION OF ALCOHOLIC LIQUORS.

PRODUCTS OF THE ALCOHOLIC FERMENTATION AND ITS ACCOMPANYING CHANGES.

1. **Alcohol** is a limpid and colorless liquid, having a specific gravity of 0.7938 at the temperature of 60° Fahrenheit, and boiling at 173° F. when the barometer is at 29.9 inches. It is a stable and strictly definite chemical compound, represented by the formula C_2H_6O (or, in the old notation, $C_4H_6O_2$)—that is, it is composed of $\frac{24}{46}$ carbon, $\frac{6}{46}$ hydrogen, and $\frac{16}{46}$ oxygen. It enters into chemical union with but few substances, none of its combinations being in use, but it forms permanent mixtures or solutions with a large number of substances, and it is chiefly in these mixtures that alcohol is found in commerce. Thus, alcohol mixes in all proportions with water, ether, and the numerous salts of ethyl, most of the volatile oils, glycerine, and with acetic, sulphuric and nitric acids. It dissolves large proportions of the sugars, but does not dissolve the albumens, gelatines, or gums. In mixture with much water, however, it dissolves the gums, and dextrine, to a considerable extent. It also dissolves very large numbers of salts, alkaloids, colors, and other compounds.

2. The term alcohol, used as a proper name, is applied

both to the absolute substance, C_2H_6O, farther specified by chemists as **ethylic** alcohol, and to its mixtures with smaller proportions of water and slight proportions of other substances. In chemistry, the word alcohol is used as a common or generic name to designate several series of substances. A list of one of these series is given in paragraph 11. But these numerous alcohols, though having a definite chemical relation to each other, are all strictly independent and invariable substances. It is not correct to speak of methylic alcohol, or amylic alcohol, as varieties or variations of alcohol—any more than it would be to mention calomel as a variety of corrosive sublimate or saltpetre as a variety of lunar caustic. A distinct substance cannot vary in qualities.

3. With whatever other substances alcohol may be mixed, it is itself unalterable in every quality,—being neither finer nor coarser, weaker nor stronger than ethylic alcohol must always be. The **mixtures** of alcohol with other substances may present infinite variations in qualities, according to the character and the proportions of these substances.

4. Alcohol—in all its forms and mixtures known in commerce—is produced only by **the fermentation of sugar.** The formation of alcohol from the elements, through a succession of chemical changes, can be brought about in a number of ways, but these methods are far too difficult and expensive to be employed for commercial purposes. The alcoholic fermentation of sugar is chiefly a transformation of sugar into alcohol and carbonic acid gas, thus:

$$\underset{\text{Sugar, 180 parts.}}{C_6H_{12}O_6} = \underset{\text{Alcohol, 92 parts.}}{2C_2H_6O} + \underset{\text{Carb. ac. gas, 88 parts.}}{2CO_2}$$

This transformation takes place only in presence of living

yeast, a plant growing in the shape of slightly attached egg-shaped cells (Torula cerevisiæ) not over $\frac{1}{250}$ inch (0.1 millimetre) in diameter. The substance of the plant is nitrogenous, hence some admixture of nitrogenous material with the sugar is indispensable to the fermentation. The change occurs only in water solution not over one-fourth sugar or one-fifth alcohol, and at temperatures between 33° and 122° F., but access of the air is not essential.

5. Along with the alcoholic fermentation, small but variable portions of the sugar are resolved into **other products** beside ethylic alcohol. A portion (according to Pasteur as much as 4 or 5 per cent. of the sugar) is converted into succinic acid and glycerine, according to the following equation:

$$\underset{\text{Sugar.}}{49C_6H_{12}O_6} + \underset{\text{Water.}}{30H_2O} = \underset{\text{Succinic acid.}}{12C_4H_6O_4} + \underset{\text{Glycerine.}}{72C_3H_8O_3} + \underset{\text{Carb. ac.}}{30CO_2}$$

In most cases a portion—which under some conditions is not a very small part of the sugar—produces amylic alcohol ($C^5H_{12}O$), and traces of butylic alcohol ($C^4H_{10}O$), propylic alcohol (C_3H_8O), and other members of the alcohol series given under paragraph 11, are often formed—the result being varied by conditions. (Farther, See 7.)

6. **The sugar** for the alcoholic fermentation is glucose, or grape sugar, also named starch sugar, and it may be derived from a multitude of sources. The juice of nearly all fruits contains sugar; starch, the largest constituent of all the cereal grains and of potatoes, is easily transformed into sugar; and woody-fibre is changed to sugar by action of sulphuric acid. The change of starch into sugar is effected by hot dilute mineral acids, and also by

the saccharine fermentation which is induced in the germination of seeds, in the digestion of starch-food, and by the conditions of alcoholic fermentation. In each case, the starch first becomes dextrine, which changes to sugar. Cane sugar and milk sugar change to glucose by action of the alcoholic ferment.

$$\underset{\text{Starch.}}{C_6H_{10}O_5} + \underset{\text{Water.}}{H_2O} = \underset{\text{Glucose.}}{C_6H_{12}O_6}$$

$$\underset{\text{Sucrose.}}{C_{12}H_{22}O_{11}} + \underset{\text{Water.}}{H_2O} = \underset{\text{Glucose.}}{2C_6H_{12}O_6}$$

$$\underset{\text{Woody-fibre.}}{C_6H_{10}O_5} + \underset{\text{Water.}}{H_2O} = \underset{\text{Glucose.}}{C_6H_{12}O_6}$$

7. Under the action of certain ferments, sugars are converted into lactic acid, and by persistence of the same conditions lactic acid is converted into butyric acid. The following equations represent these—the **lactic** and **butyric fermentations:**

$$\underset{\text{Sugar.}}{C_6H_{12}O_6} = \underset{\text{Lactic acid.}}{2C_3H_6O_3}$$

$$\underset{\text{Lactic acid.}}{2C_3H_6O_3} = \underset{\text{Butyric acid.}}{C_4H_8O_2} + \underset{\text{Carb. ac. gas.}}{2CO_2} + \underset{\text{Hydrogen.}}{4H}$$

The natural ferment which induces these changes is a fungus termed Penicillium glaucum, composed of cells not over $\frac{1}{10000}$ inch (0.0025 millimetre) diameter, with branching cells grouped together. Accompanying the alcoholic fermentation from starch in grain and in potatoes, and of sugar in grape juice and beet juice, there frequently occurs a production of traces of other **volatile fatty acids** belonging to the same series with butyric acid,—as caproic acid ($C_6H_{12}O_2$), œnanthic acid ($C_7H_{14}O_2$), caprylic acid ($C_8H_{16}O_2$).

8. When alcohol diluted with water is exposed to the air at warm temperatures, or is subjected to other oxidizing agents, it suffers two degrees of oxidation, resulting in the **formation of acetic acid** (which also belongs to the same series with butyric acid). These changes, which are not true fermentations but correspond to combustion and decay, are defined as follows:

$$\underset{\text{Alcohol.}}{C_2H_6O} + \underset{\text{Oxygen.}}{O} = \underset{\text{Aldehyd.}}{C_2H_4O} + \underset{\text{Water.}}{H_2O}$$

$$\underset{\text{Aldehyd.}}{C_2H_4O} + \underset{\text{Oxygen.}}{O} = \underset{\text{Acetic acid.}}{C_2H_4O_2}$$

In ordinary acetification—the alcoholic liquid containing albuminoid matters—the oxidation of the alcohol is accompanied and greatly accelerated by the presence and growth of an organized ferment, the "vinegar plant," or Mycoderma aceti, a fungus composed of spores having a mean length of $\frac{1}{800}$ inch and thickness of $\frac{1}{1700}$ inch (0.031 by 0.015 millimetre). The other members of the alcohol series—given in paragraph 11—are liable to oxidation like that of ethylic alcohol, each producing an aldehyd and each aldehyd producing an acid, these acids constituting a homologous series of acids—those given with the acids in 11. Hence, by action of the air during the alcoholic fermentation, certain minute portions of the various alcohols named in paragraph 5 may be transformed into the volatile fatty acids mentioned in 7.

9. By the action of acids upon alcohols, **ethers** (and water) are produced, as follows:

$$\underset{\text{Ethylic alcohol.}}{C_2H_5HO} + \underset{\text{Acetic acid.}}{HC_2H_3O_2} = \underset{\text{Acetic ether.}}{C_2H_5\,C_2H_3O_2} + \underset{\text{Water.}}{H_2O}$$

$$\underset{\text{Ethylic alcohol.}}{C_2H_5HO} + \underset{\text{Butyric acid.}}{HC_4H_7O_2} = \underset{\text{Butyric ether.}}{C_2H_5\,C_4H_7O_2} + \underset{\text{Water.}}{H_2O}$$

In this manner, during the **ageing of wines and liquors**, are formed small quantities of acetic ether, butyric ether (pine-apple essence), œnanthyc ether (Hungarian wine oil), pelargonic ether, acetate of amyl (pear oil), valerianate of amyl (apple oil), and other fragrant ethers.

10. Under certain conditions sugar undergoes the viscous or **mucous fermentation,** with formation of gum and mannite:

$$\underset{\text{Sugar.}}{25C_{12}H_{22}O_{11}} + \underset{\text{Water.}}{13H_2O} = \underset{\text{Gum.}}{12C_{12}H_{20}O_{10}} + \underset{\text{Mannite.}}{24C_6H_{14}O_6} + \underset{\text{Carb. acid.}}{12CO_2}$$

This change sometimes occurs in fermented liquors, causing ropiness. It takes place in presence of an organized ferment, composed of spherules $\frac{1}{18000}$ to $\frac{1}{21000}$ inch (0.0014 to 0.0012 millimetre) in diameter, the spherules mostly cohering in chains and the chains interlaced together.

11. The following table comprises the compounds known at present as members of **The Ethylic Series of Alcohols and the Acetic Series of Fatty Acids.**

	ALCOHOLS.	$C_nH_{2n+2}O$	BOIL.	ACIDS.	$C_nH_{2n}O_2$	BOIL.
1	Methylic..	CH_4O	150° F.	Formic....	CH_2O_2	221° F.
2	Ethylic ...	C_2H_6O	173° "	Acetic.....	$C_2H_4O_2$	243° "
3	Propylic ..	C_3H_8O	205° "	Propylic...	$C_3H_6O_2$	284° "
4	Butylic ...	$C_4H_{10}O$	233° "	Butyric ...	$C_4H_8O_2$	314° "
5	Amylic....	$C_5H_{12}O$	270° "	Valerianic.	$C_5H_{10}O_2$	347° "
6	Caproic ...	$C_6H_{14}O$	299° "	Caproic....	$C_6H_{12}O_2$	392° "
7	Oenanthic.	$C_7H_{16}O$	327° "	Oenanthic.	$C_7H_{14}O_2$	?
8	Caprylic ..	$C_8H_{18}O$	356° "	Caprylic...	$C_8H_{16}O_2$	457° "
9	....	.....	....	Palargonic.	$C_9H_{18}O_2$	500° "
10	Rutic.....	$C_{10}H_{22}O$	....	Rutic	$C_{10}H_{20}O_2$	......
11	....	....	....	Euodic....	$C_{11}H_{22}O_2$	......
12	Lauric....	$C_{12}H_{26}O$	....	Lauric	$C_{12}H_{24}O_2$	......
13	....	....	....	Cocinic....	$C_{13}H_{26}O_2$	......
14	....	....	....	Myristic...	$C_{14}H_{28}O_2$	......
15	....	....	....	Benic	$C_{15}H_{30}O_2$	......
16	Cetylic....	$C_{16}H_{34}O$	....	Palmitic...	$C_{16}H_{32}O_2$	......
17	....	....	....	Margaric ..	$C_{17}H_{34}O_2$	......
18	....	....	....	Stearic....	$C_{18}H_{36}O_2$	......
19	....	....	....	Balenic....	$C_{19}H_{38}O_2$	......
20	....	....	....	Butic	$C_{20}H_{40}O_2$	......
21	....	....	....	Nardic	$C_{21}H_{42}O_2$	......
27	Cerylic....	$C_{27}H_{56}O$	....	Cerotic....	$C_{27}H_{54}O_2$	......
30	Melissic...	$C_{30}H_{62}O$	....	Melissic...	$C_{30}H_{60}O_2$	......

CONSTITUENTS OF THE ALCOHOLIC SPIRITS AND LIQUORS OF COMMERCE.

12. The "**alcohol**" **of commerce** is of different grades, being ethylic alcohol with admixture of **water** in proportions ranging from 7 to 16 per cent. by weight as ordinary limits, and with "**fusel oil**" (15) in proportions which vary from an indistinguishable trace to an amount largely altering the odor of the mixture. Traces of aldehyde and of acetic acid are often present. The "Alcohol" of the U. S. Pharmacopœia is 85 per cent., by weight, of pure alcohol, a grade not much used. The "Stronger Alcohol, or Alcohol Fortius" of the U. S. Pharmacopœia—the ordinary best druggist's alcohol—is 92 per cent. by weight of pure alcohol.* The "absolute alcohol" of commerce is not such in fact, but contains 4 or 5 per cent. by weight of water, with scarcely any fusel oil. "Anhydrous alcohol" is the term applied to an article which is chemically pure, or nearly so. See Table at paragraph 53.†

13. "**Proof Spirit,**" as designated by the U. S. Government, is 50 per cent. by volume at 60°, or 43 per cent., by weight, of pure alcohol. Proof Spirit in Great Britain is

* The alcohol most extensively sold is from 89 to 92 per cent. by weight, being called "95 per cent. alcohol" with reference to measure by volume.

† The addition of **ether** as an adulteration in commercial alcohol —to lower specific gravity and compensate for water—has been reported (1).

(1) SHUTTLEWORTH: Canadian Pharm. Jour., July, 1873, p. 420.

56 per cent. by volume, or 49 per cent. by weight, of alcohol.

14. The **Distilled Liquors** in commerce contain, as legitimate constituents:

Alcohol,—from the proportion in British proof spirit, defined above, down to about 30 per cent. by weight. The U. S. Pharmacopœia requires whiskey and brandy to havo from 48 to 56 per cent. by volume (41 to 49 per cent. by weight) of alcohol.

"**Fusel Oil.**" In the most carefully distilled liquors, not present in quantities sufficient to be easily identified, but in the larger number of liquors it can be found, in proportions varying from an ineffective trace to an amount notably affecting the sensible properties of the liquor.

Ethers, acetic acid, volatile oils,—as specified under the head of each liquor—in very small quantities, slightly affecting the odor and flavor.

Color-substances and astringents from the wood of casks —minute quantities.

Water—being the remainder of the liquor.

Farther—as **additions** and not legitimate—we may find the various articles mentioned in the description of liquors below, and others that the caprice or ingenuity of the manipulator may suggest.

15. Fusel oils consist of those products of the alcoholic fermentation which distil at a temperature higher than the boiling point of ethylic alcohol. Whatever the field of the fermentation, the chief of the fusel-oil products is amylic alcohol: while butylic and propylic alcohols and the volatile fatty acids may severally be present in variable but subordinate quantities. See 5, 7, and 11. Potato-fusel-oil, corn-fusel-oil, the fusel-oil from the marc of grapes, and that from beet-root possess characteristic differences. Potato-fusel-oil is almost wholly amylic alcohol; grape-fusel-oil contains more butylic alcohol and is especially rich in the volatile fatty acids. In fermentation, raw grain is productive of more fusel-oil than malted grain, and potatoes more than grain; the expressed juice of fresh grapes forms but little and the marc of grapes a good deal; but the conditions are as influential as the materials. As separated and sold, fusel-oils always contain ethylic alcohol.*

16. The principal **distilled liquors** are whiskey, gin, rum, and brandy.

Whiskey is the diluted alcohol distilled from fermented grain (malted or not) or potatoes. That from malted grain is at highest price and contains least fusel-oil (with

* RABUTEAU deduced from experiments with frogs (**L'Union**, 1870, 90; **Schmidt's Jahrbuecher Gesam. Med.**, 1871, B. 149, p. 264) that Amylic Alcohol produces poisonous effects closely resembling those of Ethylic Alcohol, but of fifteen times greater intensity. The frogs were floated in a 0.002 solution of the alcohol (1 part to 500 parts of water) and then in stronger solutions, and the effects of depressed action of the heart, congestion, anæsthesia, and death were timed. Amylic alcohol produced the same effects in the same times as did ethylic alcohol of 15 times greater concentration, or butylic alcohol of 3 times greater concentration. From which it was inferred that the poisonous action of butylic alcohol is 5 times more intense than that of ethylic alcohol in same quantity. Rabuteau also exper imented with himself by taking 0.25 to 0.50 grammes, (4 to 8 grains) of amylic alcohol in a glass of wine, and the results **confirmed** the conclusions given above.

On the other hand, observers of cases of delirium tremens and acute alcoholism, have not found it more likely to result from use of cheap grades of spirits with much fusel-oil than from purer **and stronger** grades. (Alcoholism in Russia, HERMANN.)

equal care in distillation). In old whiskey, traces of the acetates and valerianates of ethyl and amyl are formed (9) and color and a very little tannic acid are derived from the cask.

Originally, whiskey was distilled by direct application of a strong heat, whereby the solid residues of the wort undergo some destructive distillation and a smoky odor and flavor are imparted to the liquor—(some fusel-oil being also distilled over). At present, the smoky odor is obtained, if at all, by the addition of a drop or two of **creosote** to the gallon of malt spirits. It is sometimes directed to add one or two drops each of creosote and purified fusel-oil to the gallon! But the most of the spirit termed whiskey is not characterized by a smoky odor. For **color,** burned sugar (caramel), logwood, catechu, tea infusion, etc., are sometimes added. There is no evidence that strychnia has ever been used in the making up of whiskey, or other distilled liquor, and no probability that it will be so used. Its intentional addition to the malt-wort could only arise from gross ignorance, and would not at all affect the distillate; and its addition to the distilled liquor would be an expensive measure, promising to lessen rather than increase the market price of the beverage. As to use of strychnia in beer, see 48.

Methylic alcohol, derived from distillation of wood, and known as wood spirit, wood naphtha or pyroxylic spirit—with some creosote left from the crude wood spirit—is perhaps sometimes added to whiskey. The British Government permits spirit one-ninth methylic alcohol to go free of tax—as being secure against use as a beverage.

17. Gin is grain spirit flavored with oil of **juniper** or oil of **turpentine,** or both. Formerly, in the distillation, juniper berries (or Strasburg turpentine) were placed in the retort. At present, oil of juniper is added in proportion of about one fluid-ounce of the oil to 33 gallons of spirit, or oil of turpentine in proportion of about one fluid-ounce to 10 gallons of spirit. The manufacturers of gin make this addition of oil of juniper or of turpentine to grain spirit—with water, common salt, and other slight additions peculiar to each manufacturer—and re-distil an amount somewhat exceeding that of the grain spirit taken. Among the slight **additions** characterizing the several brands of manufacture are oils of lemon, bitter almonds, caraway, cassia, sweet fennel, and cardamoms; creosote, garlic, and horseradish root. Potassa is said to be sometimes added, to give "piquancy" prized by the lower orders of gin drinkers in England, but it is rarely or never actually found by analysts. Veritable gin, if faithfully redistilled from water and common salt—the water being about one-half the quantity of the grain spirit taken—contains far less fusel-oil than whiskey, indeed should not contain enough to be readily found at all. Cayenne pepper and sulphate of zinc are mentioned as additions by dealers, and sugar is frequently added in considerable quantity. Color is not added to gin, and care is taken that it shall not receive much color from casks. Also, a little acetic acid is sometimes added to diminish color. Holland gin, distilled from juniper, was introduced as Schiedam Schnapps, a name since applied to various gin-mixtures.

18. Rum was originally distilled from fermented juice of sugar cane (which is 12 to 16 per cent. sugar), and is now made to some extent from the residues and skimmings of sugar manufacture, but is mostly made of grain.

spirit with flavoring additions. **Butyric ether** (pineapple oil) is the characteristic flavor added to rum. Butyric acid also is often added, and with the dilute alcohol it forms butyric ether. The flavor is sometimes obtained by adding sliced pineapples to the spirit. The "rum essence," prepared to add to grain spirit and make rum, is made up of various substances, including many which are also used in "brandy essence."

19. Brandy, in the strict meaning of the term, is the dilute alcohol distilled from fermented grape juice, and, hence, contains the volatile constituents of wine. Veritable brandy, unless from wine taken in part at least from fermented marc of grapes, cannot contain much fusel-oil; and (like other distilled liquors) if distilled with care it must be free from notable proportions of fusel-oil. On the contrary, if improperly distilled, from fermented marc, it may contain much fusel-oil. As wine fusel-oil is comparatively rich in acids (7), especially in œnanthic and pelargonic acids, the formation of the **ethers** of these acids (9) is correspondingly abundant. Hence age produces more effect in brandy than in other distilled liquors. **Artificial brandy** is a grain spirit with additions of substances which are characteristic constituents of a grape spirit. It may be made more or less nearly identical in composition with veritable brandy. Fictitious brandy is a grain spirit with additions which make it resemble a grape spirit in flavor and odor rather than in composition. A substitution for brandy is a grain spirit (in most cases), not modified to approximate grape spirit, but merely presented as such. The term brandy, as used in commerce, without qualification, must be held by common consent to include artificial brandy.

20. The **ethers** characteristic of old grape spirit are formed by the volatile acids of the acetic series, especially œnanthic acid and those contiguous to it in the series, and acetic acid, these acids being in combination with ethyl chiefly and in smaller proportion with amyl. A little free acetic acid is always, and aldehyde is usually present. The ethers **added,** in artificial brandy, are chiefly **acetic ether** and the "œnanthic ether," or "**pelargonic ether**" of commerce, also termed "Hungarian oil of wine." This is a somewhat variable mixture of several ethers, being ethyl compounds of the fatty acids between the 5th and 10th of the acetic series, artificially prepared from various materials. (11). In fictitious brandy, the **spirit of nitrous ether** (sweet spirits of nitre) is much used for the cheaper grades, often with **aromatics** and other substances, of which a great variety are employed. Higher priced brandies are formed of grain spirit by acquiring age after the addition of "oil of wine," "oil of grapes," or the "eau-de-vie de marc." The "oil of wine" used for this purpose is, approximately, the ethereal oil of the pharmacopœias, containing ethylene and ethyl sulphate: the "oil of grapes" is the fusel-oil last distilled from fermented marc of grapes or from lees of sour wine, then etherized with sulphuric acid, and contains amyl sulphate. "Eau-de-vie de marc" is the unchanged fusel-oil and spirit distilled by a quick fire from lees of sour wine or from fermented marc of grapes. **Tannic acid** in some form is generally added in artificial and fictitious brandies, and often in proportion larger than can be derived from the cask by very old brandy. Veritable brandy is of course colorless when new, but it has become customary to give artificial and fictitious brandies a **color** deeper than the pale yellowish tint derived by long standing in the cask. Caramel is the color most often employed, but other colors are used, as mentioned under the head of Whiskey (16).

21. The following are some examples of brandy making. "Brandy essence,"—15 parts of acetic ether, 12 parts of spirit of nitrous ether, 1 part of rectified wood spirit (16). "Brandy essence,"—5 parts of oil of grapes, 4 parts of acetic ether, 1 part of tincture of all allspice, 3 parts of tincture of galls, 100 parts of "alcohol." Take 1 part of either of these "brandy essences" to 1,000 parts of "alcohol," with 600 parts of water. Or,—2,500 to 3,000 parts of 80 to 90 per cent. alcohol, 1,700 to 2,000 parts of water, 10 parts of spirit of nitrous ether, 5 parts of tincture of allspice, 1 part of acetic ether, 2 parts of tannic acid. (The spirit of nitrous ether contains 5 per cent. or less of ethyl nitrite.) A London "brandy improver:" acetic ether, oil of capsicum, sugar, and caramel. The oils or tinctures of cassia and cloves, and oil of bitter almond are used.

22. Under the name of **liqueurs**, or cordials, are included a great number of special and proprietary drinks, consisting of grain spirit usually somewhat more dilute than ordinary distilled liquors, with a great variety of aromatics, frequently heavily sweetened and sometimes brightly colored—violet, green, blue, or of other tint. Anilin colors (possibly containing arsenic), and other colors of doubtful safety are liable to be used.

Absinthe is a liqueur with 40 to 60 per cent. by volume of alcohol and several per cent. of volatile oils—those of wormwood (artimisia **absinthium**), cinnamon, cloves, anise, and angelica being chiefly used. It is slightly colored green with fresh leaves of spinach and parsley. It has been colored with acetate of copper, also with a mixture of indigo and gamboge.

23. Of the **alcoholic drinks not distilled,** those most in use are fermented from grape juice and from grain: wines and beers.

24. The juice of grapes, or **must,** contains from 10 to 30 per cent. of sugar; from 0.5 to 1.5 per cent. of free acid (calculated as tartaric acid), chiefly tartaric acid and acid tartrate of potassium, with variable or slight proportions of racemic, malic, and citric acids; tannic acid; 0.2 to 0.8 per cent. of albumen; small quantities of gum, pectine, wax, and fat; "extractive matter;" and 0.25 to 0.40 per cent. of mineral substances—potassium, sodium, calcium, magnesium, aluminum, iron, manganese, phosphates, chlorides, sulphates, and silica—the potassium salts and phosphates predominating. During and after fermentation, there is a separation of "argol" or crude "cream of tartar" chiefly the acid tartrate of potassium, with some tartrate of calcium, and traces of other salts.

Wine, the fermented juice of the grape without additions, contains:

(a) Alcohol, 7 to 20 per cent. by weight:

(b) Non-volatile Substances, 3 to 10 per cent., including

Grape Sugar, 0.1 to 3.0 per cent., (in a few varieties of wine, 10, 13, 14 per cent.);

Free Fixed Acid equal to 0.3 to 0.6 of tartaric;

Tannic Acid, usually 0.08 to 0.20 per cent.;

Glycerine, 0.1 to 0.5 (maximum 2.0) per cent.;

Albumen (usually less than in must as given above, the nitrogen ranging from 0.02 to 0.06 per cent.);

Gum, Pectine, Fat, Wax, Color,—(all in the must);
Ash, 0.17 to 0.27 per cent. (phosphoric anhydride 0.04 to 0.06 and potassium oxide 0.09 to 0.13 per cent.; potassic phosphate fully two thirds the ash);
Tartrate of Ethyl, decomposed upon evaporation;

(c) Volatile Substances beside alcohol and water,—
Ethers, mentioned in 9;
Fusel-oil (See 15);
Acetic Acid (0.06 to 0.12 per cent.).

It will be seen that the (b) contents of wine comprise all the substances of must—with a great reduction of the amount of sugar, a diminution in the slight amount of albumen, an abstraction from the acid and the ash of the amount of "argol" formed, and with the addition of glycerine and formation of tartaric ether,—while there is in wine an addition of (a) and (c) contents not in must. The Free Acid consists of tartaric acid and its isomers and acid tartrate of potassium, with frequent inclusion of malic or citric acid, or both, and succinic acid. Tartaric acid may suffer decomposition, to a slight extent, during fermentation. A small portion of the tartaric acid becomes neutralized in tartaric ether, not volatile like the other ethers, but on evaporation decomposed to leave tartaric acid. Tannic acid is scarcely found at all in white wines.

The **color-substance** of red wine is chiefly Oenocyanin or Oenocyn ($C_{10}H_{10}O_5$), blue-black when pure, insoluble in water, alcohol, or ether, but soluble in dilute alcohol acidulated with tartaric or acetic acid, being turned red by acids, while fixed alkalies restore its blue color, and ammonia changes it first green, then brown. Its spectrum shows no absorption bands, but a general absorption increasing toward the violet. The yellow tint of "white wines," is derived from oxidation of "extractive" and is similar to that found in humus.

25. The most frequent **additions to must**, or fermenting wine, are the following:

Sugar,—to increase the alcoholic strength of wines which otherwise would be weak. (CHAPTAL's method. But not over about 20 per cent. by weight of alcohol can be obtained by fermentation).

Sugar and water,—to reduce acidity or to increase the product. PETIOT's plan is the addition of sugar and water to the water-washings of expressed grapes.

Alcohol,—to "strengthen" or to preserve the wine. After fermentation it may be added to amount to more than the 20 per cent. by weight.

Glycerine is named among the additions by wine makers in Europe, as proposed by Scheele in 1865, from 1 to 3 per cent. being the proportion added.

Calcined **Gypsum,**—to prevent viscous fermentation (10) or restore ropy wine, to fix color, to remove water. It is also sometimes sprinkled upon the grapes. Wine of ordinary alcoholic strength will hold in solution about 0.08 per cent. of gypsum—of greater alcoholic strength a smaller quantity—increasing the amount of sulphates in the ash. **Alum** is sometimes added to deepen and fix color, and will remain in solution.

Sulphites and sulphurous acid may be named here—though usually added after fermentation, if at all. Casks are often treated with the vapor of burning sulphur. These additions—designed to prevent mouldiness and check acetification--by gradual oxidation furnish sulphates and possibly sometimes free sulphuric acid in the wine.

The result last named can occur when the sulphurous acid or acid sulphite is added in such excess as to form a quantity of sulphuric acid greater than the bases can neutralize.

Marble dust—to neutralize and remove excessive acidity of must after fermentation. If not added in undue quantity, it only increases the amount of argol and proportion of calcium in the same, without leaving calcium in solution; but if added in excess, calcium salts remain dissolved.*

Neutral tartrate of potassium is added to reduce the free acid of wine, which it does by increasing the deposition of acid tartrate of potassium. If added in excess, it remains in the wine, increasing the residue of solids and the ash.

Gelatine, or gum arabic, with tannic acid, are sometimes added in clarifying must and excess of gum or tannic acid may remain in solution.†

Vegetable red **colors.** Juice of elderberries (sambucus canadensis and nigra) and of bilberries (vaccinium myrtillus).

26. Diseased or "sour" wines—produced chiefly by the fermentations described in paragraphs 8, 7, 10—are turbid and often ropy and usually contain an undue quantity of acetic acid. According to Hager,‡ if more than 0.2 per cent. of acetic acid is found, the wine may be declared diseased. This amount of acetification does not occur unless the action of the air is aided by the contact

* Chaptal's Method—report of Moschini and Sestini upon—Jour. Chem. Soc., vol. xi, 1275; from Gazetta chimica italiana, iii, 195.

† 3 oz. of tannin are enough for 1200 litres of wine; after about a week add a solution of isinglass.—**Bayerischer Bierbrauer,** 1872.

Parent—**Ding.** polytech. Jour., 201, 4 (1872)—recommends addition of tannin for conservation of wines.

‡ **Untersuchungen,** II, 316.

of the vinegar plant, the cells of which can be found, as described in 7, much smaller than those of the yeast plant. Wine which has become **bitter** contains an alga, composed of knotty, ramified, crumpled bodies, not over $\frac{1}{12000}$ inch (0.002 millimetre) in diameter, and with small spherical bodies interspersed. **Ropy** wine contains the spherules described in 10. The amount of tartaric acid is somewhat reduced by acetification in wine.

27. The discrimination between certain similar wines, and the estimation of the commercial value of the finer wines, is to a considerable extent dependent upon the trained sense of smell and taste of an expert. But, though flavor and odor are varied by differences not determined by the chemist, the effect which the wine has upon the system varies more with the proportions of its chief constituents, and is most plainly indicated by a chemical analysis.

28. The **artificial production of wines** is not, like that of brandy, a task which chemical skill can hope to accomplish. Beside the great complexity of the ethers, the solid "extractives" are requisite. Then, the peculiarity —in many cases the commercial value—of an actual wine depends upon certain proportions of the constituents named above, which proportions the chemist cannot fully determine. The ethers of wine elude quantitative analysis. Moreover, there are doubtless substances in wine not identified. It may be perfectly true that a mixture of pure alcohol, water, glucose, bitartrate, and ethers may be made in such carefully adjusted proportions that it will probably be capable of producing whatever effect wine would produce upon the system ; and, indeed, may be less objectionable for administration, more agreeable, and (when offered as wine) more salable than are many grades of actual wine, yet such a mixture is not actual wine, and should not be presented as such.

29. It is not possible to specify all the materials which enter **the fictitious wines of commerce**, or which, in all parts of the world, are added to actual wines. And the additions to wines assume all proportions—from a slight correction of the must to the taking of a gallon of actual wine in the make-up of a barrel of a liquid to be called wine.

30. The **alcohol** employed in making-up wines is usually ordinary grain spirit, while that added to must is strong alcohol, and the higher priced wines are sometimes fortified with brandy. In the majority of cases, the distilled spirit used contains much more **fusel-oil** than average wines contain.

31. There is no occasion to add **free acid** to grape-juice wines for acidity. But sulphurous acid or sulphuric acid may have been added as a preservative. In addition to what is stated on this point in paragraph 25, the statement of Graeger should be considered, viz., that free sulphuric acid results from reaction between gypsum and acid tartrate of potassium in wine, when gypsum is dusted upon the grapes or when water containing calcium sulphate is used, with sugar, in Petiot's process.* Now **sulphuric acid**, and **alum**, are very common additions in fictitious wines, but as we have seen, either may be added in a grape-juice wine. Nevertheless, more than minute proportions of either must be accepted, at the least, as an unwarrantable sophistication.

32. In the making-up of wines, for **acidity**, bitartrate

* **Dingl. polyt. J.**, ccvii., 430, and **Jour. Chem. Soc.**, 1873, 957.

of potassium and tartaric acid are most employed, lemon-juice perhaps sometimes. Wine casks are coated with argol by rolling them while containing a little hot saturated solution of bitartrate of potassium. **Cider** is a prominent constituent of many "wines," (especially port and champagne). The apple-juice has about the same proportion of free acid that must contains, the predominant acid being malic. In cider calcium predominates; in grape wine magnesium is more abundant than calcium (110). The "wine" made up from the juice of "pie-plant" (Rheum Rhaponticum and other varieties of Rheum) contains **oxalic acid** and acid oxalates.

33. Fictitious wines are often made more **astringent** than veritable wines: tannin, catechu, rhatany, kino, oak shavings, and logwood being used—the two last named for purpose of color.

34. **Sugar** is a usual constituent of made wines; commonly cane-sugar, which, however, by presence of free acid, gradually changes to grape-sugar. Presence of cane-sugar may be regarded as evidence of sophistication or substitution.

35. The **color** of fictitious wines is obtained by addition of various articles, including logwood, elder-berries, and danewort, brazil-wood, bilberries, privet berries, mulberries, holy oak flowers, red poppy, litmus, red saunders, oak sawdust, caramel, and anilin colors.* (See 100 **g. h.** etc.). Alum is much used to deepen color, especially that of elder-berries.

* E. B. Shuttleworth reports, in the Canadian Pharmaceutical Journal, 1874, June, p. 381, finding fuchsine in a sample of "port wine." Also, that he has ascertained that a mixture of magenta and "azaline" is sold extensively to color made-up wines. See 100 *l*.

36. Almonds, oil of bitter almonds (artificial ? *), tincture of grape-seed, cloves, and various volatile oils and aromatics are used—in minute quantities—to make up a flavor.

37. The odor or bouquet of wines is attempted by use of pelargonic, acetic, and butyric ethers, sweetbrier, orange flowers, orris root, etc.

38. It has been for a long time reported that **lead** oxide, or granulated lead, is sometimes added to wines to lessen acidity or to check acetification; also that acetate of lead has been directly added for that purpose. Traditions and recipes directing these additions have been and may now be astray among the ignorant, and may be executed; but probably lead is more likely to occur in wine from contact with lead-spigots, shot left from cleaning bottles, or use of lead pipes. Storer found lead in a wine containing also free sulphuric acid—the plumbic sulphate being probably held in solution by alkaline tartrates and sulphates.† Zinc, tin, and copper may occur in wines accidentally, as just stated of lead, by solution of the metals, and arsenic as a constituent of zinc vessels, or of sulphuric acid or anilin.

39. Beer (including Ale and Porter) is the liquid obtained by fermentation of malted grain, without concentration or dilution, and consists of the constituents of malt soluble in water, with a little hop, as altered by the alcoholic fermentation and to a slight extent by acetification

* Nitrobenzole, now largely substituted for the natural oil of bitter almonds as a perfume and a flavor, is an active poison, a few drops constituting a poisonous dose.

† Chem. News, xxi, 16, (1870, March).

and (often) lactic fermentation. **Malt** is grain first germinated and then roasted: in germination some of the starch is changed to dextrine, and a little of the dextrine to sugar, by the saccharine fermentation, the gluten being in part also modified to diastase, and in roasting, another portion of starch is changed to dextrine, sugar is changed to caramel (caramelin, etc.), and assamar and "extractives" are formed. Concerning the fermentations just mentioned, see paragraphs 4 to 8, inclusive.

40. Pale malt is dried at temperature not above 100° F. and used for the palest ales; amber-colored malt, at 120° to 125° F.; brown malt, for porter, at 150° to 170° F.; black malt, used only for coloring, at 360° to 400° F.

41. The alcoholic fermentation, for ales, porter, and the most of the beers except "lager-bier," is conducted at temperatures ranging from 60° to 90° F.; British pale ale, not above 72° F. The Bavarian beer (lager-bier or stored beer) is fermented at temperatures below 50°, and then stored at a temperature near the freezing point of water. For example, in a brewery at Heidelberg, the wort was fermented for 8 or 9 days at 41° to 46° F. and then stored for 8 to 12 months at 34° to 36° F.

At low temperatures, the yeast grows by atmospheric oxidation of the gluten; the alcoholic fermentation is retarded until nearly all the gluten is destroyed, and in consequence of the absence of gluten (and low temperature) little acetic acid is formed in the beer. The moderate evolution of carbonic acid gas carries no scum to the surface, the yeast sinks to the bottom as fast as it is formed, and such yeast, called bottom yeast (Unterhefe), reproduces this form of fermentation, called sedimentary fermentation (untergahrung). On the other hand, at high temperatures, the gluten is oxidized at expense of some decomposition of sugar to sustain the yeast [LIEBIG], the alcoholic fermentation is completed when gluten remains undecomposed in the beer, and from presence of gluten (and high temperature) acetic acid is formed. The tumultuous evolution of the gas carries the yeast to the surface, where it remains, and this yeast—top yeast (Oberhefe)—will again favor this variety of fermentation, called superficial fermentation (Obergahrung). (See table on next page.)

The weight of pale to amber (dry) **malt** averages 92 per cent. of anhydrous barley, or nearly 80 per cent. of barley in its natural condition (containing 12 or 13 per cent. of water). The loss is chiefly carbonic anhydride and dust of celluline.

The albuminoid matter of beer includes **yeast cells.** The average proportion of nitrogen in yeast is about 10 per cent. (9 to 12 per cent.)—the nitrogen in albumen varying (between much narrower limits) from 15 to 16 per cent.

43. The **proportion of hops** added varies from 0.5 per cent. to 2.0 per cent. of the malt, by weight: (German draught beer, 0.6 to 1.0 per cent.; German stored beer, 1.3 to 2.0 per cent.).

The bitter and oil and extractive matter of hop remain in solution: the tannic acid is precipitated by the albuminous constituents of malt wort and is left behind. The bitter substance constitutes 4.7 per cent. of the hop strobils, and 0.9 per cent. of the lupuline or 5.1 per cent. of the entire hops; the Volatile Oil constitutes 0.12 per cent. of the strobils, or 0.11 per cent. of the entire hops; the strobils forming 0.9 and the lupuline 0.1 of the hop.

42. *Average Composition, per centum.*

CHIEF CONSTITUENTS.	Barley.	Amber Malt.	Malt-wort.	Scotch Ale.	English Porter.	German Draught Beer.	German Lager Beer.
Alcohol	....	....	....	8.0	5.5	3.2	4.3
Water	12.0	....	....	....	....	....	....
Organic Solids	86.0	97 5	12 to 20	10.5	6.0	5.0	4.5
Starch	65.0	47.0	5 to 9				
Dextrine	1.5	12.0	1.3 to 2.2	4.6 to 4.8—average.—GSCHWANDLER.			
Glucose	0.5	1.0	0.1 to 0.2	0.2 to 1.9.—PRANDTL.			
Albuminoids	10.0	10.5	1.1 to 1.8	About 0.5 to 0.7.			
" nitrogen of	....	....	....	0.047 to 0.125.—A. VOGEL.			
Fat	2.0	2.5	....				
Glycerine	....	....	....	Estimate: 0.05 to 0.25 (1)			
Caramel, Assamar, Glucic acid.	....	} 14.5					
Extractives	....		1.5 to 2.5	1.8 to 3.7 (estimated from malt).			
Celluline	7.0	10.0	....				
Acetic, Lactic, and Succinic acids	....	....	....	0.14 to 0.32 Acetic; 0.15 to 0.50 total.			
Carbonic anhydride	....	....	....	0.15 to 0.17			
Ash (2)	2.0	2.5	0.2 to 0.4	0.6	0.4	0.2	0.3
Hop bitter and hop oil	....	....	....	0.026 to 0.105 (estimated from manufacture.)			

(1) This estimate is made, in ratio of alcoholic contents, from the amount of glycerine found in wines.
(2) The ash of beer is nearly one-third potassa, fully one-third phosphoric anhydride, and one-third silica and earths.

44. Cane sugar is sometimes added to malt wort, and in Great Britain this addition is permitted by law. By this means the proportion of alcohol is increased without increase in the solids.

45. Common salt is frequently added in the fermentation of malt wort, so that the ash of beer is rich in sodium and chlorine, only traces of which are present in the ash of malt.

Alkaline carbonates are sometimes added to correct "sour" beers. It is held that over 0.075 per cent. of alkaline carbonate (0.750 gramme in 1 litre) indicates sophistication in German beer,* but it is evident that the richest ales may normally contain as much as 0.2 per cent. (2.000 gramme in 1 litre).

46. The following may be farther named as the most frequent unauthorized (fraudulent) **additions to beer.** As bitters—quassia, gentian, wormwood (artimisia absinthium), aloes, buckbean (menyanthes trifoliata), "herb bennet" or "blessed thistle" (centaurea benedictus). As aromatics, —anise, fennel, cinnamon, coriander, caraway, cardamom, ginger, capsicum. Sulphate of iron (ferrous), alum, and **sulphuric acid** have been used,—the former two to impart frothiness, the latter to simulate age and alcoholic strength.

Caramel, generally in the crude form of empyreumatic burned sugar, and with the common name "essentia bina," has a limited but not infrequent use in making up beers.

Tartaric acid with alkaline carbonates is much used to form carbonic acid in light and cheap sorts of beer. There is at this time (1874) a report in the journals that **colchicum** seeds are being used as a substitute for hops in beer in Germany.

* **Hager's Untersuchungen, II, 324.**

47. There is scarcely a doubt but that the **cocculus indicus** has long been, and continues to be employed to some extent in beer, both in Great Britain and in this country, although the evidence for this opinion is mostly presumptive rather than positive, and is mostly based on the existence in commerce of a quantity of the drug much larger than there is other known use for. Also, there are various second-hand reports of its purchase by brewers. It is, however, used to intoxicate and kill fish.*

So early as the reign of Queen Anne of England it appears among the substances which brewers were forbidden to use.

48. There is scarcely any evidence that **strychnia** or nux vomica has ever been added to beer.†

In 1850, it became reported in Great Britain that strychnia was extensively used in ales,—the report being afterward traced to a surmise of M. Pelletier, the celebrated manufacturer of quinia, etc., at Paris, who had received an unusually large order for strychnia to go to England. By direction of the Analytical Sanitary Commission, Messrs. Graham and Hoffman made analyses of forty samples of new and old ales obtained from various places. The samples, however, were all of the two largest ale manufacturers, Allsopp & Sons, and Bass & Co.,—whose ales had come in question and who had asked for

* Correspondence relating to the use of cocculus indicus.—Phar Jour. and Trans. Vol. IV., 3d Series.

† A. CASSELMANN examined a beer called Bayrischer quass, at Petersburg. It had a clear brown color, acid reaction, and very bitter taste. Picric acid and aloes were not present. The extract by animal charcoal, was extracted from residue with alcohol and then with ether after alkali, and the result gave clear reactions for strychnia.—**Hager's Untersuchungen**, II., 327.

the examination. Graham and Hoffman found no traces of strychnia in the forty samples; their method being competent to give clear indications when a gallon of beer contained as much as half a grain of strychnia.*

The intentional addition of strychnia to beer by the manufacturer or dealer, as a supposition, is certainly improbable, though less absurd than the adulteration of whiskey with strychnia (16). Not being an immediate stimulant or intoxicant, the only purpose it can serve is due to its bitterness, as a substitute for hops. Now, though intensely bitter, it is still more intensely poisonous, so that it is not possible materially to increase the bitterness of beer by strychnia without rendering it, in the liberal doses in which it is drank, so violently poisonous that the adulteration would commonly be discovered, to the great danger of the vender. Hassall has stated that it requires not less than three grains of acetate of strychnia (free acetic acid being present in beer) to give "a suitable and persistent bitterness" to a half a gallon of water, and hence not less than one and a half grains of strychnia as acetate are needed to furnish any material increase of bitterness in half a gallon of beer. Nevertheless, one grain of strychnia, not acetate, renders six gallons of water "perceptibly" bitter. One grain of strychnia is a full fatal dose; one-half grain has produced a fatal result, and will at least cause violent symptoms of acute poisoning. Therefore, the drinking at one sitting of one to two pints of beer rendered "suitably" bitter by strychnia would, according to Hassall's data, in most cases bring the beverage under immediate legal investigation. Moreover, the effects of strychnia accumulate in the sys-

* Hassall's Adulterations, p. 516.

tem for hours and days, and the symptoms of its poisonous action are distinctive and well known. The bitter taste of strychnia is unlike that of hops, its intensity increasing and becoming an unpleasant metallic bitter aftertaste.

The cheapness of strychnia favors its attempted use, as it is sold by dealers at a rate not over half a cent per grain. Farther, there is no physical difficulty in its being held in solution in beer. It has indeed been stated* that the tannin from hops in beer would throw strychnia wholly out of solution. But we have seen (43) that the tannin acid of hops does not remain in beer. Moreover, the insolubility of tannate of strychnia in 20,000 parts of water is by no means assured, and with the solvent action of acetic acid, as in beer, is quite improbable.

49. Picric acid (trinitrophenic acid) has long been named among the adulterations of beer, but without good evidence, and its use is now deemed by all authorities to be improbable.

* Ure, in his **Dict. Arts, Manuf., and Mines**, I, 165 (Appleton's edition).

THE CHEMICAL EXAMINATION OF ALCOHOLIC LIQUORS.

50. Ethylic alcohol is identified by its sensible properties (**a**); by the production of iodoform (**b**); by the production of acetic ether (**c**); by certain deoxidizing effects (**d**). If pure or mixed only with an equal or smaller proportion of water, alcohol will be recognized by its odor, and other sensible properties: if otherwise impure, before testing for its identification, it should be separated by fractional distillation—collecting in the receiver only that portion of the distillate formed while the thermometer in the retort stands at 173° to 212° F. However, many substances more or less volatile are carried over by adhesion to alcohol vapor, and very odorous substances in this way continue to cover the odor of alcohol after repeated distillations.

a. When sufficiently separated, alcohol is a colorless, limpid liquid, with a characteristic **odor**, penetrating and somewhat agreeable.

b. When, in presence of alcohol, iodine is warmed in contact with fixed alkali, **iodoform** is gradually produced as a light yellow, crystalline precipitate. First iodate is formed and then it is reduced (and joined with iodine) to iodoform, thus:

$$6KHO + 6I = KIO_3 + 5KI + 3H_2O$$

$$KIO_3 + C_2H_6O + 2I = CHI_3 + KCHO_2 + 2H_2O$$

Now, if there is not proportionately enough water present, the yellow precipitate of iodoform may be covered by a white one of iodate, insoluble in the alcohol not yet decomposed. This (white) iodate precipitate may afterward change to iodoform, or for lack of free iodine it may remain unchanged. Therefore, the reagents should be used in definite proportions, as follows: a solution of iodide of potassium in 5 parts of water, just saturated with iodine, and a 10 per cent. solution of hydrate of potassium.

Take 3 to 5 c. c. of the distillate to be tested; 5 to 6 drops of the potassa solution; warm to 100° to 120° F. (38° to 48° C.), and add of the iodine solution, in drops, slightly agitating after each drop, till the liquid is brownish yellow. If, on standing a short time the iodine color does not disappear, add, by drop, of the potassa solution till nearly or quite colorless. If the alcohol is only in traces, iodoform will only appear after standing. It crystallizes in pale yellow, scaly particles: under a power of 200 to 400 diameters these are seen as well-defined **hexagonal** stars and rosettes.

Acetone, aldehyde, acetic ether, amylene, and butyric alcohol also yield iodoform in this test. Ether, acetic acid, chloral and its hydrate, chloroform, and amylic alcohol do not yield iodoform by this test. According to Lieben (whose name is given to the test), methylic alcohol does not respond to this test,* but the earlier statement that methylic alcohol also yields iodoform is retained in many recent works. The samples of wood spirit in commerce yield iodoform abundantly.

c. To a portion of the distillate or material to be tested in a test-tube, add one-third its volume of sulphuric acid and a drop or two of acetic acid or solution of acetate, warm gently and set aside to cool. If alcohol is present,

* Annal. der Chem. und Pharm., suppl. B. vii., 137.

the characteristic, penetrating, agreeable odor of **acetic ether** will be apparent. Ether responds to this test.

d. Alcohol slowly **reduces** chromic acid to (green) chromic oxide, in hot solution. The chromic acid may be taken from potassic dichromate and hydrochloric acid. The alcohol as distilled, may be passed in vapor into (a little of) the reagent by a delivery tube dipping therein. Or, liquid alcohol may be digested with the reagent. But this reaction is common to aldehyde, acetic acid, formic acid, and some other volatile, as well as many non-volatile bodies.

Permanganate of potassium solution is but very slowly and gradually reduced—the red color turning slightly paler and brownish—by action of pure ethylic alcohol (distinction from methylic alcohol which quickly decolors the solution).

Nitrate of silver solution is not darkened or disturbed by pure alcohol (free from aldehyde and from the tannic acid derived from casks).—But after distillation from a very little dichromate and sulphuric acid, the distillate—containing **aldehyde** and acetic acid—will quickly reduce metallic silver from the nitrate.

Alkaline cupric solution is not reduced by alcohol. Pure alcohol (free from tannic acid) does not darken after addition of an equal volume of stronger water of ammonia.

51. Ethylic alcohol is determined quantitatively by first separating it from all other substances except water, by distillation; then finding the specific gravity (or the boiling point) of the mixture of alcohol and water, and lastly consulting tables which give the proportion of alcohol in its aqueous mixtures of different degrees of specific gravity (or of boiling point). Distillation is necessary before determination of alcohol in "distilled liquors" and "alcohols" of commerce, unless they are proven free from fusel-oil and other extraneous material; and (distillation or evaporation) is inevitably necessary in the case of fermented liquors.

The **absence of water** is shown if a few grains of (white) anhydrous cupric sulphate upon a porcelain surface are not immediately turned bluish when the alcohol is dropped upon it.

The distillation should be so conducted as actually to accomplish the separation from all other substances except water. If the spirit or liquor taken has an acid reaction (which may be due to a volatile acid), it must be carefully neutralized with caustic alkali. The bulk of the distillate should never be less than the bulk of the liquid taken, and when the greatest exactness is required, twice the bulk of the original liquid should be distilled,—enough water being always added to the contents of the retort so that the residue of distillation shall measure not less than one-fourth or more than one-half the bulk of the original liquid. For most practical purposes, a distillate of equal bulk and a residue of one-third bulk may be relied upon and obtained as follows: Fill the specific gravity bottle accurately at standard temperature with the alcoholic material, wipe the rim and stopper, pour the contents into the retort and rinse the bottle with distilled water two or three times into the retort, taking in all water enough to fill the bottle one-third full. Then distil into the specific gravity bottle till it is very nearly full and adjust the temperature and add water accurately to fill it. If greater exactness is desired, distil to fill a bottle exactly twice the capacity of that in which the original liquid was measured, adding to the retort water enough twice to fill the smaller bottle.

Fifty cubic centimeters (1.7 f. oz.) is a sufficient **quantity of material,** if weights for the specific gravity can be taken on a good chemical balance.

The **heat applied** in distillation should be limited to 212° F., the steam or water bath being most convenient.

To **prevent frothing** of wines in the retort Griffin recommends the addition of a little tannic acid in the retort—about one grain to two fluid ounces.

52. The proportion of alcohol is most often stated for specific gravity at 60° F. (15⅝° C.). Other temperatures are also employed. There are slight differences between different authorities; as it is scarcely possible to attain absolute exactness, and even the separation of anhydrous alcohol has been approximated with varying closeness. The figures of the following tables give results sufficiently near for all practical purposes. In the use of a table having water at its maximum density, 4° C. (as Tralles') for the unit of specific gravity; or water at 0° C. for the unit (as Delezenne); the water contents of the specific gravity bottle should of course be weighed at the temperature of the unit. In the first of the two following percentage tables, the temperature of the water unit is 59° F.; in the second, 60° F. The last column of the second percentage table is to be understood as follows, for example: a bottle which would hold 1.0000 parts by weight of water at 60° F., would hold 0.9986 parts of water at 77° F., or 0.9106 parts of fifty-per-cent. alcohol at 77° F.—provided that the bottle was no larger at 77° than at 60°. As the bottle is larger at the higher temperature, for the utmost exactness a correction may be made for this difference.

This may be done by use of the proportions given in the following table by Dr. Pile, (the cubical expansion of glass being $\frac{1}{38700}$ = 0.0000258 for each 1° C. between 0° and 100° C.).

Temp. F.	*Apparent Sp. Gr. in glass bottles.*	*True Sp. Gr.*
59°	1000.07	1000.08
60°	1000.00	1000.00
61°	999.92	999.91
62°	999.84	999.82
63°	999.72	999.72
64°	999.68	999.63
65°	999.60	999.53
66°	999.51	999.43
67°	999.42	999.33
68°	999.33	999.23
69°	999.24	999.12
70°	999.14	999.01
71°	999.04	998.90
72°	998.94	998.78
73°	898.83	998.66
74°	998.72	998.53
75°	998.60	998.40
76°	998.48	998.27
77°	998.35	998.13

53. Percentage of Alcohol, by Weight and by Volume, and of Water by Volume, for Specific Gravity at 15°C. (59°F.),—Water at same temperature being the unit.

STAMPFER'S Table. From HAGER'S *Untersuchungen*, II, 295.

Specific Gravity.	Percentage. By Weight. Alc.	Percentage. By Volume. Alc.	Percentage. By Volume. Water.	Specific Gravity.	Percentage. By Weight. Alc.	Percentage. By Volume. Alc.	Percentage. By Volume. Water.	Specific Gravity.	Percentage. By Weight. Alc.	Percentage. By Volume. Alc.	Percentage. By Volume. Water.
1.0000	0.	0	100.	0.9607	28.14	34	69.04	0.8954	60.38	68	35.47
0.9985	0.80	1	99.05	0.9595	29.01	35	68.12	0.8930	61.43	69	34.44
0.9970	1.60	2	98.11	0.9582	29.88	36	67.20	0.8905	62.50	70	33.39
0.9956	2.40	3	97.17	0.9568	30.75	37	66.26	0.8880	63.58	71	32.35
0.9942	3.20	4	96.24	0.9553	31.63	38	65.32	0.8855	64.64	72	31.30
0.9928	4.00	5	95.30	9.9538	32.52	39	64.37	0.8830	65.72	73	30.26
0.9915	4.81	6	94.38	0.9522	33.40	40	63.42	0.8804	66.82	74	29.20
0.9902	5.61	7	93.45	0.9506	34.30	41	62.46	0.8778	67.93	75	28.15
0.9890	6.43	8	92.54	0.9490	35.18	42	61.50	0.8752	69.04	76	27.09
0.9878	7.24	9	91.62	0.9473	36.09	43	60.58	0.8725	70.16	77	26.05
0.9867	8.06	10	90.72	0.9456	37.00	44	59.54	0.8698	71.30	78	24.96
0.9855	8.87	11	89.80	0.9439	37.90	45	58.61	0.8671	72.43	79	23.90
0.9844	9.69	12	88.90	0.9421	38.82	46	57.64	0.8644	73.59	80	22.83
0.9833	10.51	13	88.00	0.9403	39.74	47	56.66	0.8616	74.75	81	21.76
0.9822	11.33	14	87.09	0.9385	40.66	48	55.68	0.8588	75.91	82	20.68
0.9812	12.15	15	86.19	0.9366	41.59	49	54.70	0.8559	77.09	83	19.61
0.9801	12.98	16	85.29	0.9348	42.53	50	53.72	0.8530	78.29	84	18.52
0.9791	13.80	17	84.39	0.9328	43.47	51	52.73	0.8500	79.51	85	17.42
0.9781	14.63	18	83.50	0.9308	44.41	52	51.74	0.8470	80.72	86	16.32
0.9771	15.46	19	82.60	0.9288	45.37	53	50.74	0.8440	81.96	87	15.23
0.9761	16.29	20	81.71	0.9267	46.33	54	49.74	0.8409	83.22	88	14.12
0.9751	17.12	21	80.81	0.9247	47.29	55	48.74	0.8377	84.47	89	13.01
0.9741	17.96	22	79.92	0.9226	48.26	56	47.73	0.8344	85.74	90	11.88
0.9731	18.79	23	79.09	0.9205	49.24	57	46.73	0.8311	87.04	91	10.76
0.9721	19.63	24	78.18	0.9183	50.21	58	45.72	0.8277	88.37	92	9.62
0.9711	20.47	25	77.28	0.9161	51.20	59	44.70	0.8242	89.72	93	8.48
0.9700	21.31	26	76.33	0.9139	52.20	60	43.68	0.8206	91.08	94	7.32
0.9690	22.16	27	75.43	0.9117	53.19	61	42.67	0.8169	92.45	95	6.16
0.9679	23.00	28	74.53	0.9095	54.20	62	41.65	0.8130	93.89	96	4.97
0.9668	23.85	29	73.62	0.9072	55.21	63	40.63	0.8089	95.35	97	3.77
0.9657	24.70	30	72.72	0.9049	56.23	64	39.60	0.8046	96.83	98	2.54
0.9645	25.56	31	71.80	0.9026	57.25	65	38.58	0.8000	98.38	99	1.28
0.9633	26.41	32	70.89	0.9002	58.29	66	37.54	0.7951	100.00	100	0.00
0.9620	27.27	33	69.96	0.8978	59.33	67	36.51				

54. Percentage of Alcohol, by Weight, for Specific Gravity at 15.6°C. (60°F.) and at 25°C. (77°F.),—Water at 15.6°C. being the unit in both cases.

Per cent. By Weight.	Spec. Grav., Water at 60°=1.		Per cent. By Weight.	Spec. Grav., Water at 60°=1.		Per cent. By Weight.	Spec. Grav., Water at 60°=1.	
Alc.	At 60°F. (1)	At 77°F. (2)	Alc.	At 60°F.	At 77°F.	Alc.	At 60°F.	At 77°F.
0	1.0000	0.9986	34	0.9511	0.9446	68	0.8769	0.8689
1	0.9981	0.9966	35	0.9490	0.9424	69	0.8745	0.8665
2	0.9965	0.9948	36	0.9470	0.9402	70	0.8721	0.8641
3	0.9947	0.9927	37	0.9452	0.9382	71	0.8696	0.8616
4	0.9930	0.9909	38	0.9434	0.9363	72	0.8672	0.8591
5	0.9914	0.9893	39	0.9416	0.9343	73	0.8649	0.8568
6	0.9898	0.9876	40	0.9396	0.9323	74	0.8625	0.8544
7	0.9884	0.9862	41	0.9376	0.9302	75	0.8603	0.8522
8	0.9869	0.9846	42	0.9356	0.9280	76	0.8581	0.8500
9	0.9855	0.9831	43	0.9335	0.9259	77	0.8557	0.8476
10	0.9841	0.9816	44	0.9314	0.9237	78	0.8533	0.8452
11	0.9828	0.9801	45	0.9292	0.9214	79	0.8508	0.8426
12	0.9815	0.9787	46	0.9270	0.9192	80	0.8483	0.8401
13	0.9802	0.9773	47	0.9249	0.9171	81	0.8459	0.8377
14	0.9789	0.9759	48	0.9228	0.9150	82	0.8434	0.8352
15	0.9778	0.9746	49	0.9206	0.9128	83	0.8408	0.8352
16	0.9766	0.9733	50	0.9184	0.9106	84	0.8382	0.8300
17	0.9753	0.9719	51	0.9160	0.9081	85	0.8357	0.8275
18	0.9741	0.9706	52	0.9135	0.9056	86	0.8331	0.8249
19	0.9728	0.9692	53	0.9113	0.9034	87	0.8305	0.8223
20	0.9716	0.9678	54	0.9090	0.9011	88	0.8279	0.8197
21	0.9704	0.9661	55	0.9069	0.8989	89	0.8254	0.8173
22	0.9691	0.9646	56	0.9047	0.8969	90	0.8228	0.8147
23	0.9678	0.9631	57	0.9025	0.8947	91	0.8199	0.8118
24	0.9665	0.9617	58	0.9001	0.8923	92	0.8172	0.8091
25	0.9652	0.9603	59	0.8979	0.8901	93	0.8145	0.8064
26	0.9638	0.9590	60	0.8956	0.8878	94	0.8118	0.8037
27	0.9623	0.9574	61	0.8932	0.8853	95	0.8089	0.8008
28	0.9609	0.9556	62	0.8908	0.8829	96	0.8061	0.7980
29	0.9593	0.9538	63	0.8886	0.8807	97	0.8031	0.7950
30	0.9578	0.9521	64	0.8863	0.8784	98	0.8001	0.7920
31	0.9560	0.9500	65	0.8840	0.8761	99	0.7969	0.7888
32	0.9544	0.9482	66	0.8816	0.8736	100	0.7938	0.7858
33	0.9528	0.9465	67	0.8793	0.8713			

(1) Fownes, *Phil. Trans.*, 1847, pp. 250, 251.

(2) From Squibb's Table, *Proc. Am. Phar. Asso.* 1873, p. 566,—obtained by calculation from Tralles' differences for temperature.

55. Correction of per cent. of alcohol for **differences of temperature** in specific gravity may be made with approximate correctness by the following formula: The number of degrees C. above or below the temperature given in the table is to be multiplied by 0.4; the product to be added to the percentage of the table when the temperature was below that of the table, and subtracted when it was above. Thus, by the second table of percentage, a spirit of the specific gravity of 0.9416 at 15.6° C. has 39 per cent. alcohol. If at 25° C. the same specific gravity be obtained we subtract from 39 (25—15.6)×0.4 or 3.76. This gives us 35.24 as the per cent. of alcohol for specific gravity of 0.9416 at 25° C., very nearly that given in the table (interpolation for 35.24 per cent. giving specific gravity 0.94167).

56. Volume per cent. corresponding to weight per cent., and the reverse, may be calculated by the following formulæ: Let **s** be the specific gravity of the spirit under consideration; *s* the specific gravity of anhydrous alcohol at same temperature; **w** the weight per cent. of alcohol by the table (or **v** the volume per cent. of alcohol by the table). Then

$$\mathbf{w} \times \mathbf{s} \div s = \mathbf{v}$$

$$\text{and} \quad \mathbf{v} \times s \div \mathbf{s} = \mathbf{w}$$

The volume per cent. of water in a spirit is found by multiplying the weight per cent. of water (100–weight per cent. of alcohol) by the specific gravity of the spirit.

57. The examination for Fusel-oil (14, 16, 19)—especially in distilled spirits—is always an important part of the duty of the analyst, and a part requiring much care and discretion. Unfortunately, while the importance of the inquiry appertains to the **quantity** of fusel-oil, it is scarcely possible to make an **exact** quantitative determination of it, and it is itself of a variable composition. Nevertheless, it is not difficult to ascertain whether notable and objectionable quantities of fusel-oil are present, and whether such proportions constitute a slight or an excessive impurity. Experience enables the analyst to decide this question readily and certainly.

58. **Amylic alcohol** of fermentation is a colorless and transparent limpid liquid of specific gravity 0.816, boiling at 132–3° C. (270° F.). It has a suffocating odor and burning taste. It dissolves in 30 to 40 parts of water (the excess floating), and is soluble in all proportions of alcohol, ether, chloroform, benzole, petroleum naphtha, and fixed and volatile oils. It leaves an oil spot on paper. It takes fire with some difficulty, and burns with a smoky flame.

59. The recognition of fusel-oil requires that it be first **concentrated**—by evaporating off the alcohol or fractional distillation, or by separation with ether. The simplest way is evaporation of the spirit from the palm of the hand, or from a (warmed) evaporating dish or plate, and observation of the odor obtained after dissipation of alcohol vapor. More efficient concentration is secured in the distillation of the alcohol, as directed in 51, the (warm) residue in the retort being examined by observation of odor and by tests. With fermented liquors, and whenever solids, etc., are present in the residue, it is almost indispensable after removing the ethylic alcohol to distil off the fusel-oil —using a bath of paraffine or chloride of calcium—and receiving for examination the distillate formed between 110° and 133° C. (230° and 270° F.) Another and a satisfactory mode of concentration is by adding to the spirit

in a test-tube an equal volume of pure **ether** and agitating; then adding to the whole an equal volume of water—or enough (after agitation) to cause the separation of the principal portion of the ether. The ether layer contains the fusel-oil and is allowed to rise, then decanted (or taken off with a pipette) into an evaporating dish, and the ether dispelled at ordinary temperature (warming gently at the last to remove ethylic alcohol). The residue is examined for fusel-oil (also for flavoring ethers, volatile oils, aldehyde, etc.) * Concentration with ether or with benzole or petroleum naphtha may also be often applied to the **residue of distillation** with advantage.

60. The **odor** of fusel-oil is slightly irritating to the sense, somewhat disagreeable, and usually excites coughing. It is characteristic, and must be observed from a known sample (commercial amylic alcohol). The different fusel-oils (15) are recognized from each other by their differently characteristic odors, by the senses of an expert, and in this manner only.

61. The **chemical tests** for fusel-oil depend firstly and always on the identification of its chief constituent, amylic alcohol; and secondly, sometimes, upon finding volatile fatty acids.

a. When warmed with 1½ parts of concentrated *sulphuric acid*, a **red liquid**, amyl-sulphuric acid ($HC_5H_{11}SO_4$) is formed. This product is of a viscid consistence, is soluble in water and in alcohol, and is decomposed in distillation. As sugar and many other organic substances give brown to red-brown colors with concentrated sulphuric acid, the appearance of a dull red color on the

* **Duflos' angewandten, chemischen Analyse**, S. 306; from **Bottger's polyt. Notizbl.**, 1870, S. 110.

application of this test to the residue of evaporation is not an indication of any value. The test should be applied to the fractional distillate (at 230°–270° F.), when a **red** color, even if pale, is good evidence of fusel-oil.

b. When digested or distilled with *sulphuric acid and acetic acid* or an acetate, fusel-oil yields the acetate of amyl, having the **odor of pear-oil** and volatile at 133° C. (272° F.). Unless most of the ethylic alcohol be previously removed, the odor of acetic ether (50, **c**) will mask that of amylic ether. (Acetate of amyl alone represents "jargonelle pear-oil;" 30 parts of acetate of amyl with 1 part acetate of ethyl, "bergamot pear-oil").

c. When digested or distilled with *sulphuric acid and dichromate* of potassium, fusel-oil yields **valerianic acid,** recognized by its characteristic odor, and distilling at 165° C. (329° F.). Unless the ethylic alcohol has been nearly all removed, the odor of acetic acid will cover that of valerianic.

d. The **volatile acids of fusel-oil** may be detected as follows. About 30 c. c. (1 f. oz.) of the alcoholic liquor is agitated with 2 or 3 c. c. of solution of *potassa* and evaporated by very gentle heat to the bulk of 2 or 3 c.c. This residue is cooled and treated with 5 or 6 c.c. of concentrated *sulphuric acid*, when the odor of valerianic acid and butyric acid will reveal the presence of these constituents of fusel-oil (15).*

e. Amylic alcohol decolors *permanganate* solution much sooner than ethylic alcohol (50, **d**). The volatile fatty acids of fusel-oil are still stronger reducing agents, and darken *nitrate of silver*.

f. To a portion of the original spirit in a test-tube, a

* After GOEBEL. **Hager's Untersuchungen**, II., 299.

few small fragments of *iodide of potassium* are added, with gentle agitation. If the spirit contains 0.5 or 1.0 per cent. of fusel-oil, in a few minutes a distinct yellow color appears. The tint is even visible if 0.2 per cent. of fusel-oil is present. The reaction is due to the volatile acids and not to the amylic alcohol.†

g. The **quantity of fusel-oil** may be obtained approximately, by carefully separating it through fractional distillation and water washing (59). Not less than 100 c.c. in any case, and for the best results 1000 c.c. of the spirit should be distilled. The fusel-oil distillate is taken (in a test-tube or cylindrical test-glass) while the thermometer is 110° to 133° C. (230° to 272° F.) in the retort—with care to avoid the empyreumatic products which may arise from the residue if the latter temperature is much exceeded. It is also a proper precaution to redistil the aqueous portion—that formed between 98° and 110° C. (208° and 230° F.)—adding any residue after the latter temperature is attained to the previous fusel-oil distillate. The latter is now set aside for about 12 hours: after the first hour or two, if no water layer appears at the bottom, one-fourth bulk of water is added, with agitation. After expiration of the 12 hours, take out the water layer at the bottom with a narrow pipette, and weigh the remainder as fusel-oil. The use of very much water in washing fusel-oil is impracticable, on account of the sparing solubility of amylic alcohol in water and the liberal solubility of butylic and propylic alcohols in the same solvent.

62. To examine for **Methylic Alcohol** (16, 11), add a little crude animal charcoal (or powdered wood charcoal,

† BOUVIER: **Zeitschr. Analyt. Chem.**, xi., 343. Abstract in Jour. Chem. Soc., 1873, 532, 655.

and enough alkaline carbonate to neutralize any acid reaction), and distil at 65° to 74° C. (150° to 165° F.). Aldehyde may come over below that temperature—see 71. If a distillate is obtained, it is observed for the peculiar **odor** of wood spirit, and examined as follows:

a. The addition of *potassa*, and warming by immersion of the test-tube in hot water, produces a brown color if wood spirit is present. (Ethylic alcohol is turned brown only after long digestion).

b. A portion of the distillate is treated with a few drops of a very dilute solution of *mercuric chloride*, then with *potassa* solution in excess, agitated and slightly warmed. In presence of methylic alcohol the precipitate of mercuric oxide is prevented or dissolved after warming. The precipitate may be reproduced, flocculent and yellow-white—in one portion by acetic acid, in another portion by boiling. [E. J. REYNOLDS.]

c. To a small portion of the distillate add enough dilute solution of *permanganate* of potassium to give a red color and leave transparent. If methylic alcohol is present the color will turn to brown within ten minutes.

d. In a retort of about 60 c. c. capacity, distil 2 c. c. of the distillate with 2 grammes of powdered *dichromate of potassium*, 25 drops of *sulphuric acid* and 15 c. c. of water; first digesting 15 minutes and then distilling 15 c. c. Neutralize the last distillate with sodic carbonate, evaporate to 7 c. c., acidulate with acetic acid and test for **Formic Acid** by boiling with silver nitrate. If formic acid is present the silver will be reduced (72).

e. The **quantitative determination** is only approximate. It may be based on the saturating power of the (crude) Formic acid, produced as in **d**, and measured by a volumetric solution of alkali, or by treating with baric carbonate, filtering and washing, and determining the barium in solution as a sulphate.*

f. For closer separation of methylic products from ethylic products, Hager recommends the following method, based on the aqueous solubility of **methyl oxalate** and insolubility of ethyl oxalate. Place in a retort 55 grammes of crystallized oxalic acid, 35 grammes of sulphuric acid, and 25 grammes of the distillate from animal charcoal obtained below 74° C. Digest 10 hours and distil from an oil-bath at 160° to 180° C. (320° to 356° F.). To the completed distillate add 25 times its volume of water, agitate, allow to subside, and decant the clear water solution. Treat this with potassa in excess, digest in a close bottle, acidulate with acetic acid, add acetate of potassium and chloride of calcium. Wash the precipitate of calcic oxalate, dry, ignite to carbonate (adding a fragment of carbonate of ammonium) and weigh. $CaCO_3 \times 0.64$=methylic alcohol.

Concerning Pyroligneous Acid, see 77.

63. The Acids to be considered in the examination of alcoholic liquors are chiefly the following:

In Alcohols: acetic acid (64), volatile fatty acids (61d, 75).

In Distilled Liquors: acetic acid (64), its ethyl ether (70), tannic acids (86), ethers of volatile fat acids (75), ether of nitrous acid (78), sulphuric acid (89, 80).

In Wines: tartaric acid and its acid salt (82–3), total acid (81), tannic acid (86), acetic acid and ether (64), butyric acid and ether (73–4), ethers of volatile fatty acids (75), succinic acid (85), lactic acid (85), carbonic acid (88), sulphuric acid (89), sulphates (80), ethyl nitrite (78), oxalic acid (84).

* Farther,—Prescott's Proximate Organic Analysis, pp. 57, 58.

In Beer: acetic acid (64), lactic acid (85), butyric acid (73), formic acid (72), carbonic acid (88), succinic acid (85), tartaric acid (83), chlorides (109), sulphates (113).

64. Acetic acid is the only acid likely to be present in Alcohol, where it is revealed by the acid reaction (8.11). In Distilled Liquors, an acid reaction may be due to other acids as adulterations (14). In Wine and Beer, acetic acid is almost the only normal volatile acid (beside the gas carbonic anhydride and the traces of butyric and formic acids) but it has to be separated from the non-volatile acids which are relatively more abundant in wines but less abundant in beer than acetic (24c, 26, 42). Acetic ether is of frequent occurrence in distilled spirits (70).

Acetic acid—in Alcohols, Distilled Liquors, or distillates from Wine or Beer—may be concentrated for **identification** by adding fixed alkali to a neutral or slight alkaline reaction, and evaporating nearly to dryness. The residue is then tested as an acetate,—for production of acetic ether, red solution of ferric acetate, acetone, etc.—It will be observed that any acetic acid derived from **acetic ether** in the liquor will be included in this determination.

65. The **quantity of acetic acid** may be determined in alcohols, distilled liquors, or distillates from wine or beer, by volumetric method, saturating with a deci-normal solution of alkali, on the supposition that no other free acid is present. Of a solution of 4.000 grammes NaHO in 1000 c. c., each c. c. neutralizes 0.006 grammes of $HC_2H_3O_2$. (The alkali solution may be standardized by adjusting it to a deci-normal solution of oxalic acid made by weighing 6.300 grammes perfect crystals for 1000 c. c. solution).

66. The **distillation of fermented liquors for determination** of acetic acid is more nearly complete if about an equal bulk of water is first added to the wine or beer. At least four-fifths of the whole are then distilled off, with use of a paraffine or chloride of calcium bath. It is not easy to obtain the last traces of the acetic acid without danger of forming empyreumatic acids.

67. The acetic acid may be **distilled from Wine separately from the alcohol,** by neutralizing the wine with baryta, distilling off the alcohol, adding excess of phosphoric acid, and then distilling off the acetic acid.

68. Acetic acid may be determined, in the presence of the non-volatile acids of wine, **without distillation,** by forming soluble barium salt, as follows: Add pure *carbonate of barium*, in slight excess, filter and wash, precipitate the barium acetate in the filtrate by dilute sulphuric acid (with the conditions requisite in quantitative separation of barium sulphate), wash, dry, ignite, and weigh.

$$BaSO_4 : 2HC_2H_3O_2 :: 1 : 0.515$$

69. This method is employed in determining **diseased wine** as such (26). But it will be observed again that so much butyric acid and formic acid as are present will be included in the result (according to their equivalence to acetic acid)—just as they would be after distillation. Also, **succinic** acid—present in wine and beer—will mostly remain in solution as a barium salt; and the **lactic** acid of beer will be wholly included in this estimation as acetic acid,—while these two acids are excluded by distillation.

70. Acetic Ether, or ethyl acetate, is of frequent occurrence in liquors (20, 21, 24**c**, 37). It is a transparent liquid of specific gravity of about 0.93, boiling at 77° C.

(170° F.), and having a pleasant, refreshing, penetrating and slightly acetous odor. It is neutral to test paper. When heated with caustic alkalies (64) or strong sulphuric acid, it is decomposed into alcohol and acetic acid; but it can be rectified from oxide of lead. It dissolves in 12 or 18 parts of water and in all proportions of alcohol, ether, chloroform, and bi-sulphide of carbon. **Acetic ether distils** over with the first part of the alcohol of wines and liquors. It is, also, **extracted** by washing with ether, after enough water is added to throw the ether out of solution, according to the method given for fusel-oil in the last part of 59,—the ether being evaporated at ordinary temperatures, by turning the dish. Petroleum naphtha may be employed instead of the ether. Or, distillation from a water-bath at 172° F., after dilution with much water. —Acetic ether is easily recognized by its odor, unless in presence of powerfully odorous substances. It is farther identified by yielding reactions for acetic acid, being at the same time volatile and neutral to test paper before decomposition.

71. Aldehyde is very apt to accompany acetic acid—and in alcohol and distilled liquors it may be present when acetic acid is not (8, 12, 20). Acetic aldehyde is a thin, colorless, transparent liquid of specific gravity 0.800, boiling at about 21° C. (70° F.)—above which temperature it exists in alcohol in the condition of a dissolved gas. It mixes in all proportions with water, alcohol, and ether, but is separated from water by saturating it with chloride of calcium. It does not redden litmus, but it forms salts by substitution of metals for one atom of its hydrogen (C_2H_4O). The identification of aldehyde in alcohol or distilled liquors requires that it shall first be separated by distillation at a temperature low enough to leave all formic acid and methylic alcohol behind (11). Dilute the spirit to be examined, with water, till it is not over 20 per cent. alcohol; add chloride of calcium nearly to saturation; and distil from a water-bath, below 130° F. (55° C.), into an ice-cold receiver. Aldehyde has a pungent and suffocating **odor.**—*Nitrate of silver* solution is quickly blackened by aldehyde—or the reduced silver forms a mirror coating on the test-tube. *Potassa* solution turns brown on warming with aldehyde. *Nitric acid*, or chlorine water, changes it at once to acetic acid. (The presence of aldehyde in alcohol, or distilled spirits, or wine or beer distillates, causes a prompt reduction of silver and decoloration of permanganate, and must be considered in testing for Methylic alcohol and Formic acid).

72. Formic acid is not found in alcoholic liquors in notable quantities, except in diseased wines (26) or "sour" beer, or from contamination with wood spirit (62). It distils with the last of the alcohol and first of the acetic acid (for boiling point, see 11). It may be separated from acetic acid by neutralizing the distillate with sodium carbonate, evaporating at a gentle heat to near dryness, and distilling the residue with sulphuric acid at a temperature below the boiling point of acetic acid.—Formic acid has a pungent and irritating odor and an irritating effect on the skin. When free, it slowly reduces *nitrate of silver* in warm solution; when neutralized it precipitates white formate of silver, which darkens quickly on heating. *Chromic acid* not in excess is gradually turned green, and *mercuric* chloride solution is gradually reduced, by hot solution of formic acid or formate. *Ferric chloride* gives a red solution (not unlike acetate). With *alcohol and* *sulphuric acid* at a gentle heat, formic acid produces ethyl formate, an ether distilling at 55° C., and having a strong and agreeable odor like that of peach-kernels. Concerning the quantitative determination of formic acid, see 62**e**. Formate of ethyl enters into some artificial peach-essences, and as such may be used in flavoring wines and brandies (36).

73. Butyric acid—free and as ethyl butyrate—occurs only in very slight proportions as a product of fermentation (7), in wine and brandy and in beer (from lactic acid, 42). Its etherization is easy, so that in liquors it is generally combined as ethyl butyrate, except in beer. In wine there is less lactic than butyric acid, and this is mostly in ether; in beer there is less butyric than lactic acid and this is mostly free. Butyric ether is a common addition in rum (18), and not infrequent in brandy (20), and in wine (37).—Butyric acid is a colorless mobile liquid, of specific gravity 0.974, and boiling at 156° C. (314° F.). It is soluble in all proportions of water, alcohol, ether, chloroform, but not soluble in concentrated aqueous solutions of freely soluble salts. The metallic butyrates are soluble in water, those of lead and silver sparingly.—Butyric acid will be mostly **obtained** with fusel-oil, by the methods given in 59, and especially by the method given in 61**d**.—Butyric acid is identified chiefly by its **odor** and that of its ethyl ether. The free acid has the odor of rancid butter, but somewhat less offensive, and obscurely acetous. It is a moderately strong and very persistent odor, not much diminished by diluting the acid but increased by warming it. The metallic butyrates are odorless while intact. Butyrate of ethyl has the odor of pine-apple, strong and persistent. It is readily formed by digestion of alcohol, butyric acid, and sulphuric acid.

74. Butyric Ether, ethyl butyrate, (18, 37, 9), is a colorless liquid, lighter than water, in which it is very slightly soluble; but soluble in all proportions of alcohol and ether. It distils at 119° C. (246° F.), and is mostly separated with fusel-oil by the methods given in 59, yielding butyric acid by the method described in **61d.**

75. The less volatile Fatty Acids—the 5th, 6th, 7th, 8th, and 9th of the Acetic Series (11)—formed as mentioned in 8—are concerned in the examination of liquors either as constituents of fusel-oil or as sources of artificial bouquet—" Oenanthyc ether " or " Pelargonic ether "—(20). In any case they and their ethers will be separated by the same methods employed for fusel-oil (59). Their identification, as free acids or as ethers, depends upon their odors. The odor of the ethers is agreeable but slightly suffocating; that of the free acids, rancid and irritating. The ethers decompose and yield free acids when treated according to **61d.**—Artificial bouquet, in wines or brandies, may be so made and used as not to be distinguished from natural bouquet, by chemical tests.

Tartrate of Ethyl, named among the non-volatile constituents of wine, in paragraph 24, and a substance doubtless of importance to the flavor of wines, is not easily separated. It is decomposed, at comparatively high temperatures, with separation of pyrotartaric acid. It is miscible, in all proportions, with water, alcohol, and ether. From its solubility in water, it is not to any considerable extent removed by ether washing.

76. Volatile Oils constitute frequent additions to alcoholic liquors. Among these have been mentioned **juniper**

and **turpentine** in Gin (17); **aromatics** and **bitter almond oil** (nitrobenzole?) in Wines (36, 37), and Brandies (21); **stimulant aromatics** in Liqueurs (22); **pungent aromatics** in Beer (46). Also, not an "addition," **hop oil** in Beer (42 and 43).

These oils will be partly or wholly carried over in distilling off the alcohol (50), being also to some extent received with the fusel-oil (59). A satisfactory method is the extraction of the retort residue, or the distillate, or both, with ether or petroleum naphtha or benzole, according to the process given (last) in 59.—The odor is, of course, the principal means of identification, but such color-tests and other qualitative resources as are known to chemists, for identification of the individual oils in question, should not be neglected.

Oil of juniper has the composition and the sparing solubility in alcohol of turpentine oil, but does not with hydrochloric acid form a solid hydrochlorate like the latter. It deflagrates with iodine.

Oil of Turpentine forms solid hydrochlorates of camphorous odor when treated with hydrochloric acid in the cold. With iodine it turns green and detonates.

Hop Oil will partly distil with the alcohol, but a larger portion remains in the retort—with the hop bitter (105). The oil in the distillate may usually be concentrated by extraction with ether or naphtha (with addition of water). Both the oil and the bitter of hop are extracted from the retort residue by ether. The **odor** is very intense.

Oil of Bitter Almonds is not colored with nitric acid; with sulphuric acid it forms a thick crimson liquid. Exposed to the air, it forms crystals of benzoic acid. In its fresh state, it usually contains from 3 to 14 per cent. of hydrocyanic acid, but in alcoholic liquors this minute proportion must soon decompose.

Nitrobenzole or artificial oil of bitter almonds is an oily faint-yellow liquid of specific gravity 1.2, insoluble in water, soluble in alcohol, ether, and chloroform. It boils at 400° F. being carried over with vapor of water at 212° F. like most volatile oils. Digested with a little reduced iron and a few drops of acetic acid, in a test-tube, it is reduced to anilin. The latter, with chlorinated lime turns violet to red (acidulated becomes rose-red); or with dilute sulphuric acid and peroxide of manganese, in solution, forms a purple-red to rose-red color.

Many of the volatile oils are added to liquors in the natural drug or tincture of the same—as of cloves, allspice, etc. In most of these cases the oils are accompanied with non-volatile aromatics, found among the residual solids (101½).

77. Creosote, sometimes found in whiskey (16), will be separated, if at all, in the same manner as the volatile oils,—that is, with fusel-oil, best by extraction with ether or pretroleum naphtha or benzole (59). But the quantity employed is too small for extraction by ordinary methods. Creosote is a colorless or yellowish liquid of specific gravity 1.060, boiling at about 200° C. (392°F.), soluble in 60 to 70 parts of water, freely soluble in ether, chloroform, benzole, bisulphide of carbon, and pretroleum naphtha. —Very small quantities are detected by the odor. It forms a blue color with solution of ferric chloride, and a red color with nitric acid.

Pyroligneous Acid, or Crude Wood Spirit, contains methylic alcohol, acetic acid, and creosote.

78. Nitrite of Ethyl is a frequent addition to Brandies and sometimes to Wines (20 and 21, 37), and free **Nitric acid, Nitric oxide,** and **Acetic acid** result from the gradual decomposition of the nitrous ether. Nitrite of ethyl is a yellowish liquid of specific gravity 0.947, boiling at 18° C. (64° F.), soluble in 48 parts of water and in all proportions of alcohol, ether, and chloroform. The officinal spirit of nitrous ether—properly 4 or 5 per cent. of nitrite of ethyl but often much less—has a variable specific gravity of 0.837 and when of full strength boils at 63° C. (145° F.).—In distillation of liquors, the nitrite of ethyl and nitrous acid will come over with the first portion of the alcohol, the nitric acid will partly appear with the more aqueous distillate and partly with the portion taken for fusel-oil.—A nitrite, with acetic acid, liberates iodine from *iodide of potassium*, coloring starch or bisulphide of carbon. Nitric acid forms a color layer with a cold solution of *ferrous salt*. A more efficient search for nitrous ether and the products of its decomposition is made by adding to the liquor taken for examination, potassa to slight alkaline reaction, evaporating nearly to dryness (avoiding a heat above that of the water-bath near the close of the evaporation), and then testing the residue for nitrite and nitrate together, by strong sulphuric acid and solution of ferrous sulphate.

79. Ether has been found as an addition to Alcohol (12). Such alcohol (containing more water than its specific gravity denotes) burns with a luminous flame. By adding an equal volume of water and distilling at 120° to 170° F. into an ice-cold receiver, a distillate is obtained having the **odor** and solubilities of ether.

80. "Oil of Wine" and **"Oil of Grapes"** (20) are names applied to variable mixtures of ethyl and ethylene **sulphates**, boiling at 155° to 280° C. (312° to 536° F.). They are in small part obtained in the fusel-oil portion of the distillate, but mostly left behind in the retort, or decomposed before distillation. They are separated and identified as follows: Distil off all the alcohol, according to 51, limiting the heat to that of a water-bath, and extract the residue with ether, in a test-tube, as directed for fusel-oil in 59. Then evaporate off the ether, add a little solution of *chloride of barium* and evaporate to dryness. If the residue does not wholly dissolve on digestion with water, it is evidence of the presence of ethereal sulphates in the liquor taken.

81. The Total Acid in Wines (24) is determined volumetrically in the entire wine, and stated as equal to so much tartaric acid. For this purpose, a normal solution of soda is prepared (40.000 NaHO in 1,000 c. c.)—adjusting it to neutralize equal measures of a solution of 63.000 grammes of perfectly crystallized oxalic acid in 1000 c. c. (as directed for determination of acetic acid in 65). Now measure out 75 c. c. of the wine ($H_2C_4H_4O_6$=75 × 2) into a porcelain evaporating dish of 200 to 400 c. c. capacity. If the wine is very deep colored, add water, in equal measure or enough to make the margin transparent. If the wine is pale, add solution of litmus. Then add of the normal solution of alkali to the neutral point,—using red and blue litmus papers, if necessary, to fix the neutral point. The number of cubic centimetres of normal solution of alkali required is the number of tenths of per cent. (or parts in 1000) of tartaric acid and its equivalent acid in the wine. (NaHO=40) neutralizes ($\frac{1}{2}$[$H_2C_4H_4O_6$=150)].

82. HAGER gives the following method for the **approximate determination of free tartaric acid** and equivalent acid tartrate in Wine.* Take 250 c. c. wine; add alcohol if necessary to make 15 to 17 per cent. of alcohol by weight; then add, drop by drop with stirring, a concentrated water solution of 3 to 4 grammes of normal ("neutral") tartrate of potassium, and set aside, at 12° to 15° C. (54° to 60° F.), for 3 hours. The crystalline precipitate of acid tartrate of potassium is drained on a tared filter, washed first with a little dilute alcohol, and then with 90 per cent. alcohol, dried at 100° C. and weighed. The weight multiplied by 0.4 approximately equals the amount of free tartaric acid in the 250 c. c. of wine taken.

$$(2KHC_4H_4O_6 : H_2C_4H_4O_6 :: 1 : 0.4)$$

The quantity of Acid Tartrate of Potassium in Wine may be approximately ascertained by throwing it out of solution by addition of *alcohol and ether:* Place 10 c. c. of the wine in a flask, add thereto 50 c. c. of a mixture of equal measures of alcohol and ether, stopper and set aside 24 hours. Gather the loose deposit upon a filter and wash it with the mixture of alcohol and ether, also wash the crystalline crust on the inner surface of the flask with the same mixture. Transfer the filter with its contents to the flask, add about 20 c. c. of water and boil to dissolve the acid tartrate. Determine the acid power by a deci-normal solution of alkali (81). Each c. c. deci-normal solution indicates 0.0188 grammes of acid tartrate of potassium.

83. The presence or absence of tartaric acid in Wine (32) may be investigated as follows. Evaporate about 100 c. c. to dryness on a water-bath, dissolve in 8 to 12 c. c. of hot

* **Hager's Untersuchungen**, II., 311.

water, and filter through thoroughly purified animal charcoal and wash with a little hot water. Add a few drops of concentrated solution of acetate of potassium, and to the whole a double measure of alcohol, and set aside for a few minutes. If a precipitate appears, wash it upon a filter with alcohol until the washings no longer respond to Trommer's test for sugar (94). If a tartrate, when dried and separately ignited, the precipitate exhales the odor of burning sugar. (Citric acid and Malic acid when heated evolve, each, irritating and characteristic odors). The precipitate of tartrate blackens when warmed with sulphuric acid.

For detection of tartaric acid in Beer (46) the above method may likewise be employed,—adding one-fourth volume of alcohol before filtering through the animal charcoal.

84. Oxalic Acid in Wines (32) may be detected as follows. Evaporate to one-fourth measure, neutralize with ammonia, add calcium chloride solution, digest in the cold, and filter. Wash the filter with a little dilute hydrochloric acid, and then with water, and add, to the filtrate, ammonia in slight excess. If a precipitate appears, not soluble in acetic acid, it is evidence of oxalic acid.

85. Lactic Acid is in very small proportion a normal constituent of Beer (42) and doubtless often exists in Wine (7). It is a non-volatile liquid acid, all the salts of which are soluble in water. Of the normal constituents of wines and beer, it is the only non-volatile organic acid whose barium salt is soluble in dilute alcohol (or, except succinic acid, soluble in water). By this means it may with great labor be separated, but its separation has not come within the scope of analysis for practical purposes.

Also, this is true of **Succinic Acid**, a constant constituent, in small proportion, of Wines and Beer (5, 24, 42). It is a white crystalline solid, subliming in a glass matrass with suffocating vapors and deposition of lustrous silky needles. It burns in the air with a blue flame. It is soluble in water, alcohol, and in ether. Solutions of its alkaline salts precipitate ferric salts brownish pale-red, and precipitate barium salts in presence of alcohol.

86. Tannic Acid is a natural constituent of Wines (24) and to the extent that it may be derived from the wood of casks, is an incidental constituent of nearly all liquors in very slight proportion (14). Little of that of the hop is retained in Beer (43). Either by itself, or as an accompaniment of colors or aromatics, some variety of tannic acid is a frequent addition to liquors, especially to Brandies (21) and Wines (25, 33, 35). Its reactions need to be considered especially with reference to their interference with operations bearing upon other substances.

The astringent acids of Wines are tannic and gallic acids. That of oak-wood and that of hops is quercitannic acid, the physiological tannic acid of WAGNER, and which according to his authority is not a glucoside.

Tannic acids are non-volatile solids, soluble in water, alcohol, and in ordinary ether. With caustic alkalies, they form brown to black-brown solutions, decolored again by oxalic acid. They completely precipitate all solutions of salts of alkaloids,—these precipitates being more or less readily soluble in acids. They precipitate most of the heavy metals from solutions of their salts, the precipitates easily decomposed by acids. They give blue to blue-black impalpable precipitates with ferric salts. They are removed from solution by zinc oxide and cupric oxide. They precipitate starch, dextrine, and albumen, and densely precipitate gelatine. If one drop of tannic acid solution is mixed with 1 c. c. of a hundredth-normal solution of iodine (gallic acid and hydriodic acid being formed) and the mixture now treated with a drop of very dilute alkali, a bright red color will be produced.* Tannic acids quickly decolorize the red solution of permanganate, and they reduce the warm alkaline copper solution.

The glucosic fermentation of gallo-tannic acid is prevented by alcohol, and evidently cannot occur in distilled liquors. Hence, aside from the statement, above mentioned, that the oak-wood tannic acid is not a glucoside, it appears that the tannin of the cask cannot introduce sugar into distilled liquors.

87. In examination of Wine, Beer, or Distilled Spirit for tannic acid, evaporate—for qualitative examination 100 to 500 c. c., for quantitative examination 500 c. c.—upon a water-bath—to a syrup if it be wine or beer, to near dryness if it be a distilled spirit—and extract with a mixture of equal parts of alcohol and ether. Filter if not clear, evaporate to dryness, and dissolve in water.—Qualitative: the solution precipitates gelatine, colors ferric salts inky, alkalies brown, bleaches permanganate, etc., as given in last paragraph. Quantitative: **a.** Precipitate with a clear solution of normal *cupric acetate*, filter, wash with water, dry, ignite, with aid of nitric acid, to unchangable cupric oxide, cool and weigh. $CuO \times 1.304 =$ tannic acid. [After FLECK, modified by SACKUR and WOLF]. **b.** A volumetric solution of 4.523 grammes of (German officinal)

* GRIESSMAYER: **Zeitsch. Anal. Chem.**, xi., 43; **Jour. Chem. Soc.**, 1873, 95.

sulphate of cinchonia, with 0.5 grammes of sulphuric acid and about 0.1 gramme rosanilin acetate, with water to 1 litre. This solution is added to the solution of tannic acid to be determined, until the liquid (clear of precipitate) begins to become red (the anilin being previously all held in the precipitate). Each c. c. of cinchonia solution required, indicates 0.01 gramme of tannic acid. [R. WAGNER.]

88. Carbonic Acid Gas is determined in Beer (42) as follows. The beer (well preserved in close bottles) is cooled, by immersion of the bottle in ice-water, as low as 5° C., and then poured gently into a flask. The latter has been connected with a connected pair of Woulf's bottles, so as to conduct the gas from the flask through a solution of *ammoniacal chloride of barium* in each bottle. The solution is made from 2 parts chloride of barium, 3 parts solution of ammonia, 45 parts water, filtered clear before using. The connection being made, the flask is gently warmed and the moderate flow of gas continued, by increased heat, at last to boiling. The precipitated carbonate of barium is then gathered, washed, dried and weighed. ($BaCO^3 : CO^2 :: 1 : 0.2234$). The results vary a little from changes in gathering the precipitate, but vary more from differences in boiling the beer.

89. Free Sulphuric Acid (25, 31) is an indication of significance very different from that of sulphates. It is more likely to occur in Wines than in beer or spirits, and in wines the constant presence of traces of sulphate and the frequent presence of more than traces (viz., all the calcic sulphate the dilute alcohol can hold in solution), together with the presence of a large amount of solids, render the determination of free sulphuric acid somewhat difficult. The carbonizing power of the acid furnishes the most ready means of its identification.

Wet a strip of white glazed paper in the wine, immersing it several times after short intervals, and dry it in the water oven at 100° C. A brown to red color, or positive carbonization, indicates free sulphuric acid in quantity over 0.2 per cent. of the liquid.—Also [RUNGE] a bit of white sugar, with a few drops of the wine, is evaporated on a porcelain plate at 100° C. The color will not be dark brown or black (greenish-black) unless sulphuric acid is present.—The tests being applied to the wine with negative result, a small portion of it may be evaporated on the water-bath to one-half—and then to one-fourth—with repetitions of the tests.

Another method is to evaporate 200 c. c. of the wine to dryness, ignite to whiteness, and determine the sulphuric acid in the ash by ordinary gravimetric analysis, (as required in 113). Then take another 200 c. c. of the same wine, saturate with pure carbonate of potassium, evaporate, ignite, and again determine the sulphuric acid, The excess of the second determination shows the amount of free sulphuric acid in the wine—(the sulphuric acid of ethereal sulphates, if any, see 80, being subtracted).

90. The Total Non-volatile Constituents.—"The extract" of Wines and Beer includes, beside the natural fixed substances of wine (24**b**) and beer (42), the larger number of the various fraudulent additions—(wine, 25 to 38) (beer, 44 to 48).

Twenty-five grammes of Wine or beer are evaporated in a tared porcelain capsule or evaporating dish on a water-bath until the weight is constant. The dish should be cooled in a desiccator, for weighing, as the residue is very hygroscopic, especially that of beer. One or two days' time is required for the evaporation; and for the examination of contents, ash, etc., it is well to evaporate three portions simultaneously. It has been recommended to quicken the evaporation of wine by using a glycerine-bath, glycerine itself being the most volatile material to be retained in the residue.

91. In the case of all Distilled spirits, except liqueurs (22), the **finding of a residue** is often the most easily obtained and convincing evidence of adulteration. Twenty-five grammes of genuine spirit yield scarcely a weighable residue; no other than has been derived from the wood of the cask.

92. The residue of evaporation of Wine and Beer, at 100° C., consists of substances **solid** at ordinary temperature, except glycerine and lactic acid. Sugar is usually the most abundant of these substances.

93. The Sugar of the residue of Wine and Beer is most conveniently determined by a *volumetric solution of copper* (**a**), after removing all substances insoluble in alcohol (albumen, gelatine) **c**, and in the case of astringent wines removing the tannic acid (**d**) (the quantity of which is so small in most white wines that its reduction of the copper solution though prompt is too slight to cause a material error).

a. The volumetric solution of copper is made as follows:

34.65 grm. pure cryst. cupric sulphate, dissolved in about 200 c. c. water.

150. grm. neutral potassium tartrate, dissolved in about 500 c. c. of a 10 per cent. soda solution (s. g. 1.14).

Water to make the mixture measure 1000 c. c.

1 c. c. is reduced by 0.005 grm. grape sugar }
10 c. c. " " 0.05 " " " } *

If the solution deposits cuprous oxide on boiling, or has produced any deposit, it is unfit for use. The inclusion of about 100 c. c. of pure glycerine in the litre renders the solution much more permanent.

b. The determination is made as follows: Reduce the sugar solution if necessary with a known proportion of water so that it is not over ½ per cent. sugar. Take 10 c. c. of the blue solution in a porcelain evaporating dish; dilute with 40 to 50 c. c. water, and heat to boiling. Add slowly from the burette (while the boiling is maintained) the (reduced) sugar solution, till the blue color is all destroyed (and a filtered portion of the solution, acidulated with acetic acid, gives no reaction for copper with dilute solution of potassic ferrocyanide). The amount of saccharine solution added contains 0.05 gramme of sugar.

c. Wine which is but little astringent and colored, and Beer, may be prepared for determination of sugar as follows: Take 50 c. c. (or if less than 0.1 per cent. of sugar [24, 42], 100 c. c.) of the wine or beer, mix with 1½ times its volume of 90 per cent. *alcohol*, filter, evaporate the filtrate to consistence of syrup, dissolve in water and dilute to the bulk of the wine or beer—or two, or three, or five times this bulk as needful to make the liquid not over ½ or at the most 1 per cent. sugar. A second determination may be required, in order to secure a suitable degree of dilution.

d. To remove tannic acid and color, as necessary in

* ($C_6H_{12}O_6 = 180$) takes ($2\frac{1}{2}$ $O = 40$) thereby reducing ($5CuSO_4$ $[H_2O]_5 = 1247$). Then 1247 : 180 : : 34.65 : 5

case of astringent wines, precipitate the 50 c. c. with solution of *acetate of lead*, then dilute with alcohol, filter and wash, remove the excess of lead by addition of sodium carbonate solution in least excess, filter and wash, evaporate to a syrup, and make up with water as in **c.**

94. Examination for **Sugar in Distilled Spirits** (21) is suggested when a fixed residue is found, according to 91. The sugar may have been added as a part of caramel (20) the examination for which is explained in 99. If added as sugar it will probably be found mostly as **cane sugar**, though transformation to grape sugar will occur to some extent during evaporation on the water-bath after the alcohol is removed. Liqueurs (22) contain sugar, of course.

In the **qualitative test** for sugar, the copper solution (93**a**) may be used, or a drop or two of copper sulphate solution followed by excess of potassa or soda solution. If the yellow to red-brown cuprous oxide does not appear on heating to the boiling point, continue the boiling for about five minutes: a reduction taking place after continued boiling indicates **cane sugar.** In this case, add to a new portion of the liquid to be tested one or two per cent. of hydrochloric acid and boil for ten or fifteen minutes, to transform sucrose to glucose, then neutralize and test again: an immediate reduction of copper indicating cane sugar in the material taken. Now, before deciding upon the significance of a positive result of this test for sugar, it must be questioned whether tannic acid is present, and if present it must be removed as directed in 93**d**, and the test applied in its absence. (See 86. The presence of tannic acid may be ascertained by the test with ferric solution).

The **quantitative test for cane sugar** is made by treating a measured quantity of material as directed next above; then proceeding as in 93**b.**

95. Sugar may be estimated by **fermentation and determination of the alcohol.** 59 parts of anhydrous alcohol correspond to 100 parts glucose.

96. If **cane sugar is found** in Wine or Beer, it must have been added after fermentation—as sucrose is all changed to glucose by the time any considerable portion of the sugar is fermented to alcohol. The addition of sugar to Must (25) is not ascertained by analysis; unless it has been so excessive as to be inferential from the low proportion of grape acids and extract compared with the alcohol. More easily is the addition of sugar to Malt-wort (44) inferred from undue proportion of alcohol to non-saccharine solids. As to cane sugar in "wine," see 34.

The existence of cane sugar in Wine is due, in the majority of cases, to the fact that the "Wine" is a **recent** make-up which has not experienced fermentation at all—that process having been pre-natal to its parent distilled spirit.

97. The Glycerine of Wine or Beer is separated nearly pure as follows: A weighed portion of the extract is slightly moistened with water, mixed with an excess of sodium bi-carbonate, thoroughly dried and triturated, and extracted with a mixture of equal weights of anhydrous alcohol and chloroform. The solution is evaporated on a water-bath and weighed: 0.95 of its weight being taken as glycerine.

98. Caramel is an adulteration so common in Brandy (20) as almost to have gained the authority of common consent, frequent in Whiskey (16) and other distilled spirits, and in Wine (35), and as derived from dark malt a natural constituent of Beer (42), to which, however, it is sometimes added.

Caramel is a variable product, obtained by heating crytallized cane-sugar, or the dark-colored uncrystallizable syrup from cane sugar, or starch sugar, to 210°–220° C. with addition of some potassium carbonate or sodium carbonate. It consists of three related compounds, separable by different degrees of solubility in alcohol and dilute alcohol. As a whole, the caramel of commerce is soluble in a moderate proportion of water; very little soluble in absolute alcohol, and sparingly soluble in dilute alcohol—certain kinds being soluble in spirit of the strength of wine, but not wholly soluble in proof spirit. Ether dissolves little or nothing from caramel. It is divided by dialysis.

99. All the constituents of **caramel** reduce the hot alkaline solution of copper, and reduce silver from its oxide. Caramel reduces iodine in presence of water to hydriodic acid. Solution of acetate of lead precipitates caramel, removing some kinds in part, others wholly. It is, also in part, precipitated by baryta solution.

Caramel is generally **odorless**, but it may have sugar in such a condition that when warmed with alcohol it exhales the odor of "burned sugar." It generally has a strong "burned sugar" **bitter taste**, due to that constituent soluble in 84 per cent. alcohol.

In **examination for caramel**, the residue of the Distilled Spirit or Wine is extracted with 85 per cent. alcohol and the concentrated solution—filtered if necessary—is observed as to the taste and (while warm) the odor of caramel.

In examination of Distilled Spirits, the same solution (obtained from the residue by 85 per cent. alcohol) is evaporated to remove all alcohol, dissolved in enough water, and farther tested with alkaline copper solution (see 94) for the reducing power of caramel, as stated above. If cuprous oxide is reduced, it must be ascertained whether tannic acid is present—by a drop of the solution with a drop of ferric chloride solution (86)—but if present, tannic acid cannot be removed by acetate of lead solution as directed for sugar in **93d**, because of the precipitation of caramel by that re-agent. Tannic acid may be separated from caramel, in solution, by digesting at a gentle heat with freshly ignited cupric oxide, setting aside the solution for 12 hours and filtering. The filtrate will be free from tannic acid.

100. The **coloring substances which are natural constituents** of alcoholic liquors are—in Distilled Spirits and Fermented Liquors, **oak-wood color** (14); in Wine, **grape-pigment** (24); in Beer, **caramel** (40).

The coloring substances which are used as additions to alcoholic liquors are indefinitely numerous, as we have seen. (Whiskey 16, Brandy 20 and 21, Wine 25 and 35, Beer 40).

In consequence of the great number of these foreign coloring materials, and the chemically indifferent character of most of both the natural and foreign color substances, as well as because of their small proportional quantity, their chemical determination is generally difficult and sometimes impracticable. At the same time much attention has been bestowed upon the detection of colors—especially in wine.

101. The **red color substance of Wines,** œnocyn, is described in 24. Farther: (**a**) after neutralizing with carbonate of sodium, it is precipitated with solution of *sub-acetate of lead*. The washed precipitate is treated with hydrosulphuric acid gas, then washed with hot water, when the œnocyn is dissolved out with dilute *acetic acid*. On evaporating this (red) solution, the color is obtained in residue.

b. In *dialysis*, the color of genuine red wine passes through the membrane, making a red diffusate: while **logwood** and **brazil-wood** colors are but slightly dialytic and leave the diffusate colorless to pale yellow. (ROMEI and SESTINI).

c. A strip of blotting paper wet with solution of *acetate of copper*, dipped in the wine (or spirit) and dried, shows a rose-gray from the genuine color of red wine, a violet-blue from the color of **logwood.**

d. Artificially colored wines are decolorized "in five minutes" by heating 50 c. c. of the wine with 6 c. c. of *nitric acid* of specific gravity 1.41, at 90° to 95° C. (194° to 203° F.). (FANTAGGINI and COTTINI).

The decoloration is much delayed when the operation is performed in close vessels; also when alcohol, tartaric acid, or tannic acid, have been added. (SESTINI).

Certain artificially colored wines are found not to be decolored with this re-agent. (STEIN).

It is farther reported that certain pure wines are decolored by the nitric acid in half an hour. Also, that the test is practically worthless.

e. A piece of clean bleached *sponge* does not fix and retain the color of genuine red wine, after being wet with it, a distinction from foreign colors. (BŒTTGER).

f. Pour 50 c. c. wine upon about 50 grammes of *binoxide of manganese*, agitate repeatedly, and after a short time filter. If the filtrate is clear and colorless, the color was that of genuine red wine; if dark colored, the presence of foreign color substance is indicated. (FACEN).

g. The following reactions are given by ORFILA—The re-agents in solution being added to the Wine under examination:

	Alum.	*Stannous nitrate.*	*Stannic chloride.*
Bordeaux..............	dark bronze-color.	blackish-blue.	dark blue.
Burgundy..............	do.	do.	dark green-gray.
Wine with **Bilberries**.... (*Vaccinium myrtillus.*)	dark olive-green.	gray.	green.
Wine with **Elderberries**: (*Sambucus Ebulus*, or "Danewort.")	clear olive-green.	gray-green.	bottle-green.
Wine with **Logwood**....	dark color and precip.	violet.	dark brown.
Wine with **Brazil-wood**.	violet-red.	do.	dark brown-red.
Wine with **Litmus**.......	blue red.	clear blue.	dark brown.

h. According to CHEVALIER, the addition of *potassa* in slight excess in wines gives the following indications:

Genuine red wine............. color changes to bottle-green, then brownish-green to brownish-gray.

Wine with **Elderberries**....... purple.
" with **Logwood**........... reddish-purple.
" with **Mulberries**........ violet.
" with **Brazil-wood**....... red.

i. The method of JACOB consists in adding to half a drachm of wine an equal quantity of a 10 per cent. solution of *sulphate of alumina*, then adding ten or fifteen drops of an 8 per cent. solution of *carbonate of ammonium* (or carbonate of potassium—VAN ESENBECK).

Genuine red wine................	the precipitate is dull gray with more or less reddish tinge.
Wine with **Elderberries**......... (*Sambucus Niger and S. Ebulus*).	violet precipitate.
" with **Brazil-wood**..........	grayish-violet precipitate.
" with **Logwood**.............	rose-colored "
" with **Privet berries**........ (*Ligustrum Vulgare*).	brownish-violet "

j. When *gelatine* solution is added to wine, and precipitated by the tannic acid thereof (a little tannic acid being added if necessary), the œnocyn of red wine is carried down in the precipitate, leaving the wine nearly colorless. But the color of **elderberries** (Sambucus nigra and S. Ebulus), and many other artificial colors, are left in solution, in this test. (M. FAURE).

k. Color substances in Distilled Spirits are in many cases revealed by the *odor of the residue*, when warm. **Logwood** and **Elderberries** (Sambucus Canadensis) are among those colors most readily detected in this way.

l. If a Distilled Spirit has decided color while giving little or no reaction for tannic acid (with ferric solution), it is pretty good evidence that the color has not been derived from the cask.

m. SHUTTLEWORTH recommends the following as a method of examination of wine for **anilin color**. (35, **note**). To a portion of the suspected wine, in a test-tube, add an equal volume of *fusel-oil*, agitate well and allow the mixture to separate, when, if magenta be present, the supernatant layer will be more or less tinctured of a characteristic pink or purple color. Genuine port wine, when so treated, does not impart any of its color to fusel-oil. Ether may be substituted for fusel-oil, but it does not answer nearly so well.

n. As stated in 24, the color of genuine red wine gives no absorption **band** in *the spectrum*, but only a general absorption increasing toward the violet. The coloring matter of the flowers of the **purple holyoaks** (*Althæa rosa*, *Malva arborea*, *Rose tremiere*), much used in Greece to color wines, and the colors of **logwood**, and **Brazil-wood**, all give a distinct and wide absorption band in the neighborhood of D. The wine is examined in a thin tube, is diluted if necessary, and a very little alum is added. (T. S. Phipson: Chem. News, xx. [1869] p. 229).

101½. The aromatics added to Distilled Liquors and to Wines (20, 21 and 36), are often easily recognized in the residue—by taste and odor. In case of Wines, especially if rich in sugar and grape extractives, it is advisable to extract the residue with ether, or with a mixture of equal parts of alcohol and chloroform, or chloroform alone (according to the solubilities of the aromatics).

Extraction with these and other solvents also often serves to separate aromatics from the residue of Distilled Spirits.

102. The examination of the residue of any alcoholic liquor **for alkaloids** should usually be preceded by a careful separation from extractive and saccharine matter, as always in toxicological analysis. For Stas and Otto's process, see Alkaloids, in Fresenius' Qualitative Analysis; Watts' Dictionary of Chemistry, I., 125–7, Supplement, 85; Miller's Chemistry, III., 491; Wormley's Micro-chemistry of Poisons, 411; Bloxam's Chemistry, Sec. 421. The reactions of the alkaloids will be found in the foregoing and other standard works and in the U. S. Dispensatory; also in Prescott's Proximate Organic Analysis.

Bitter Substances and **aromatics** will also be separated, in many instances, along with, or in place of alkaloids,—according to their solubility in alcohol, ether, and other solvents used. If alkaloids are not the objects of the search, the process of examination should be modified, as the solubilities of materials to be separated require.

103. The examination for foreign bitters in Beer (46, 47, 48), may be conducted as follows: *

It should be borne in mind that **hop bitter** is soluble in *ether*, and will be removed by washing the syrupy residues of beer with ether,—while salicin, quassin, cnicin, menyanthin, are not soluble in ether.

Extract the beer residue with (aqueous) *alcohol* (**solution A**), and precipitate this solution with *basic acetate of lead* (**precipitate B, Hop Bitter** and resin, ¶ 43)—filter and reserve the filtrate.

Decompose **precipitate B**, in water, with *hydrosulphuric acid* gas and filter (resin being left in residue); evaporate the filtrate to dryness and dissolve the residue in *chloroform;* add water to the clear chloroform solution, and warm to evaporate the chloroform; filter from the water the precipitate of the remaining resin, and evaporate the filtrate on the water-bath to a dry residue (**the hop bitter**). This tastes bitter, dissolves in water with acid reaction, and is soluble in alcohol, ether, chloroform, and benzole. Its aqueous-alcoholic solution is precipitated (as above) by basic acetate of lead, but not by tannic

* LEVIN ENDERS: **Hager's Untersuchungen**, II., 325.

acid; and it does not form a mirror with ammoniacal nitrate of silver.

The **filtrate reserved from precipitate B** (after basic acetate of lead) is now cleared of excess of lead by treatment with hydrosulphuric acid and filtration, freed from alcohol by evaporation, and then precipitated with *tannic acid*—(**precipitate C**: various **bitters**, as quassin, absinthin, menyanthin. Also alkaloids, if present).

Precipitate C is digested with excess of *carbonate of lead*, the mixture dried, and extracted with *alcohol* (solution of bitter substances free from tannic acid); the alcoholic solution is evaporated to dryness and the residue (**D**) triturated with ether. The (clear) ether solution (**E**) is evaporated to dryness (residue contains **absinthin**—also alkaloids soluble in ether).

Absinthin (therefore) is not precipitated by subacetate of lead, but is precipitated by tannic acid and is soluble in alcohol, in much water, and in ether. A portion of the dry residue, mixed with a drop or two of concentrated sulphuric acid and after a few moments diluted with a little water, colors blue-violet. Its water solution, boiled with ammoniacal nitrate of silver solution, form a mirror; but does not reduce alkaline copper solution. (22, 46).

That part of residue **D** not dissolved by ether as **E** is now dissolved up by warm water with alcohol. This solution (from **D**) contains menyanthin, quassin, cnicin. (Possibly Picrotoxin; see 104).

Menyanthin (from the buckbean, 46) is an amorphous, yellow semi-solid, of neutral reaction, bitter taste, sparingly soluble in cold water, freely soluble in hot water and in alcohol, not soluble in ether or chloroform. The hot saturated water solution becomes milky on cooling.

In concentrated sulphuric acid, it dissolves at first with a yellow-brown color, afterward turning violet; the water dilution of the mixture causing the separation of gray flocks. It reduces ammoniacal solution of silver nitrate.

Quassin (from quassia, 46) forms colorless columnar crystals, soluble in 200 parts water at ordinary temperatures, easily soluble in alcohol, very sparingly in ether. It dissolves colorless in cold concentrated sulphuric acid, and the addition of water to this mixture causes separation of quassin nearly unchanged.

Cnicin (from "blessed thistle," 46), crystallizes in silk-lustrous colorless needles; nearly insoluble in cold water, easily soluble in alcohol, but slightly soluble in ether. It is colored red by concentrated sulphuric acid, and this color is changed to violet on the subsequent addition of water, or to yellow by addition of ammonia. Concentrated hydrochloric acid dissolves it with a green color.

104. Picrotoxin, the active principle of the **cocculus indicus** (47), crystallizes from pure solutions in stellate groups of needles, from colored and impure solutions in interlaced spongy threads. It is inodorous, intensely bitter, neutral in reaction, and non-volatile. It dissolves in about 200 parts of cold or 50 parts of hot water, in 3 or 4 parts of hot alcohol, in 250 parts of ether, and freely in chloroform, bisulphide of carbon, petroleum naphtha, and in amylic alcohol. Concentrated sulphuric acid dissolves it saffron-colored, with slow decomposition on heating. If a trace of bichromate of potassium be added to the cold sulphuric acid solution, a violet to brown color appears: the brown color caused by adding more of the bichromate. It readily reduces alkaline copper sulphate solution.

It is removed, from acid as well as from alkaline solutions, by much ether, by chloroform, benzole, and amylic alcohol. Hence it is likely to be in part, or wholly removed in extracting for aromatics according to 101, or in cleansing the acid solution with ether in Otto's Stas' process for alkaloids. Animal charcoal takes it up to some extent, but does not hold it long against solvents.

For the **extraction of picrotoxin from Beer,** many methods have been given.

a. That of Schmidt (J. pr. Chem. lxxxvii., 344; Watts' Dictionary, iv., 644) is as follows: The liquid suspected to contain picrotoxin is concentrated over a water-bath to a syrup, diluted with water to a mobile liquid; the solution agitated with (5 or 6 grammes of) animal charcoal, after several hours filtered, and the filtrate completely precipitated with basic acetate of lead and filtered. The (wine-yellow) filtrate is then treated with $\frac{1}{20}$ to $\frac{1}{10}$ of *amylic alcohol*, shaking repeatedly, and after 24 hours the oily layer is decanted. The small remaining portion of picrotoxin may be extracted from the water liquid by repeating the treatment with amylic alcohol. The extract is left to evaporate in a warm place; the residue is boiled with water acidulated with sulphuric acid; the acid liquid is decolorized by filtration through purified animal charcoal, and evaporated till it is distinctly bitter. It is then repeatedly extracted with ether; and the ether-solution, with addition of a little alcohol, evaporated. By repeatedly dissolving the residue in weak alcohol and evaporating, the picrotoxin may be obtained in tufts of fine silky crystals. According to Schmidt, it crystallizes far better from alcohol than from ether or amylic alcohol.

b. BLAS (**Chem. Centr.**, 1872, 441 and 442; **Jour. Chem. Soc.**, 1873, 94) gives the following (shorter) method. Four to six litres of beer are evaporated to one or two litres, treated with carbonate of sodium in slight excess, and when cold agitated with its $\frac{1}{10}$ volume of ether—to remove hop bitter and other bitter substances. [Blas states that ether does not remove picrotoxin from alkaline solutions: a statement which Hager declares to be an error]. After removing the ether layer, the liquid is acidified and again and repeatedly washed with *ether*. The united ether washings are evaporated; and the (bitter) residue is dissolved in alcohol acidulated with a drop of acetic acid. The (filtered) solution is evaporated on watch-glasses, and if necessary recrystallized until distinct crystals are obtained. The needle-tufts of picrotoxin are fan-shaped or sheaf-like aggregations.

c. KOHLER gives a process wherein the beer is precipitated by acetate of lead after adding ammonia, the lead removed from the filtrate by hydrosulphuric acid, the filtrate thereof concentrated to a syrup, acidulated with acetic acid and extracted with ether. The residue from the ethereal extract is recrystallized from alcohol, as necessary.

From the chemically indifferent character of picrotoxin, **a physiological test** is a valuable means of confirmation. BLAS recommends its administration to *fishes* for this purpose (**Chem. Centr.**, 1872, 441 and 442; Jour. Chem. Soc. 1873, 94). Place, in 2 litres of water, two fishes of about 200 grammes weight, and add a portion of the purified solution or crystals to be tested. If picrotoxin is present, the fish soon turn on their backs and die. 2 grammes of cocculus indicus, corresponding to 0.1 gramme picrotoxin, is enough to kill a fish of 200 to 300 grammes weight in 10 hours. At least 6 litres of beer should be worked for the physiological test. Lupuline and hop extract do not poison fish.

105. Hop bitter (43) **may be separated from Beer** (as indicated in 103) by concentrating and washing with ether. It is also precipitated by solution of basic acetate of lead, better after extracting with alcohol, as in obtaining precipitate **B,** Enders' process, 103.

If beer is evaporated on a water-bath to one-third volume, and when warm supersaturated with common salt, the characteristic odor of the hop (also the odor of some of its substitutes) becomes unmistakable.

Concerning the hop oil, see 76.

106. For the **extraction of aloes from Beer** (46), the dry residue (of about 200 c. c.) is treated with warm dilute alkali (ammoniacal water), filtered, and the filtrate when cold is saturated with hydrochloric acid. The precipitate is gathered—(the resin of aloes). This is recognized by its characteristic **odor**; and by its solubilities and reactions, as follows: Aloes-resin is insoluble in cold water, in ether, chloroform, benzole, petroleum naphtha, bi-sulphide of carbon: is soluble in alcohol, aqueous alkalies, and hot glycerine,—also in a not too dilute water solution of aloes extractives.

The hot water solution of aloes (or the filtrate from the resin, as above) gives a (yellowish-gray) curdy precipitate with acetate of lead solution.—If the filtrate from this precipitate is freed from lead by addition of much excess of dilute sulphuric acid and filtration, then boiled for an hour with dilute sulphuric acid, and, when cold, extracted with ether, crude paracumaric acid is obtained. The ether residue is purified once or twice by solution in hot water and evaporation to crystallize. The alcoholic solution of the crystals, with very dilute ferric chloride, strikes a dark gold-brown color. Also, the same reaction may be obtained from the more impure paracumaric acid formed when the water solution of aloes extractives is boiled for an hour with very dilute sulphuric acid.

107. If examination is to be made for strychnia in beer (48), it may be done (after HOFFMANN and GRAHAM) as follows: The beer is filtered through enough animal charcoal to decolorize it; the animal charcoal is washed once or twice with a little water, then taken from the filter and boiled with alcohol and filtered hot, this being repeated with another portion of alcohol. The alcoholic filtrates are evaporated to dryness, the residue treated with solution of potassa and ether. The residue from the ether extract is tested for strychnia reactions.

108. The Ash of alcoholic liquors is obtained, in the usual way, by ignition of the residue. 100 c. c. to 500 c. c. of Wine or Beer should be taken. The addition to the residue of a few drops of strongest nitric acid—repeated from time to time, after cooling—greatly facilitates the combustion to a white ash. If **chlorides** are to be determined, the residue should be only carbonized, by a gentle ignition, and the coal extracted with hot water.

109. The **amount of ash** in Wine is given in 24; in Beer, in 42. The additions increasing the ash of Wine: gypsum, alum, sodium as sulphite, calcium as carbonate, potassium as tartrate, (25), heavy metals (37). The additions increasing the ash of Beer; common salt and sodium carbonate, (45); alum, ferrous sulphate, sodium carbonate (46); heavy metals, as lead, zinc, tin, by accidental solution by acid—(as mentioned for wine in 37).

The additions causing an ash to be obtained from distilled spirits: potassa or soda (17); copper in absinthe (22); lead as acetate (38).

Arsenic as mentioned in 38.

110. The **preponderance of magnesium over calcium in grape Wines,** and the preponderance of calcium over magnesium in Cider and "fruit wines," have been taken as a means of detecting mixture and substitution (32). But before conclusions are decided upon these grounds, the possibility of calcium having been added to grape wine, as sulphate or carbonate (25), must be considered.

On adding to 9 parts of Wine, 1 part of *ammonia*, after a few hours, "fruit wine" gives well formed microscopic tabular crystals of calcic phosphate, adherent to the sides of the vessel. They are soluble in acetic acid, and precipitated by oxalate of ammonium. The filtrate from this oxalate is not precipitated by ammonia. On the other hand, with grape wine, a white powdery precipitate (of ammonio-magnesic phosphate) falls to the bottom. Under the microscope, the crystals are seen to be star-shaped. The crystals, dissolved in acetic acid, give a very slight precipitate with oxalate of ammonium, and when this is filtered out, the filtrate is precipitated by ammonia.*

Fruit wine yields between 0.11 and 0.40 per cent. of carbonate of lime in the ash; grape wine never above 0.049 per cent. [TUCHSMIDT].

111. **Aluminum, iron,** and manganese exist in very minute proportions in the grape. The **presence of aluminum,**

* **Chem. Centr.,** 1872, 153.

with sulphates, in Distilled Spirits or in more than traces in Wine and Beer,—indicates **adulteration with alum.** According to Hager, even 0.01 per cent of aluminum (with 0.05 per cent. of sulphuric acid) in wine authorizes the suspicion of the addition of alum.

The residue of 100 c. c. of wine is ignited and the ash digested several hours with an excess of potassa in dilute solution; the filtrate therefrom being then treated with excess of chloride of ammonium. The precipitate is aluminum hydrate with traces of aluminum phosphate.

112. In like manner, the presence in the ash of notable proportions of **iron**—with sulphuric acid—indicates adulteration with sulphate of iron,—more likely to occur in Beer (46).

113. The **sulphuric acid of the ash** must be determined and considered in deciding as to additions of gypsum, or alum, or green vitriol, or sulphites, or the still more serious addition of free sulphuric acid. The solution of the ash in dilute hydrochloric acid is used in the ordinary gravimetric determination. Considerations as to the sources and significance of sulphates and sulphuric acid in Wines are made in 31, and elsewhere as there referred to. As to free sulphuric acid, see for examination, 89.

114. The examination of Wine or Beer for **arsenic, lead,** or other metal, should be commenced by the removal of organic matter,—according to usual processes for examination in cases of suspected poisoning. See Fresenius' Qualitative Analysis, sec. 225; Wormley's Micro-chemistry of Poisons; Taylor on Poisons; etc.

Dragendorff recommends the following methods of examination of beer for foreign bitters.*

* **Archiv der Pharmacie** [3], iii., 295, and iv., 389. The abstract

I. 600 to 1000 c. c. (1 to 2 pints) of beer are evaporated on the water-bath to a syrupy consistence, and then treated with 3 to 4 volumes of alcohol, as free as possible from fusel-oil, and the mixture allowed to stand 24 hours. The whole is then filtered; the alcohol is distilled off from the filtrate, and the residual liquid, after standing 12 to 20 hours in the cold, is filtered again. A few drops of dilute sulphuric acid are then added, and the whole is agitated (1) with petroleum naphtha; the supernatant petroleum layer is washed with water, filtered through a dry filter to remove the last traces of water, and left to evaporate to dryness on several watch-glasses. The aqueous acid liquor left below the petroleum naphtha is then in like manner washed (2) with benzole, and afterward (3) with chloroform, when it is made alkaline by addition of ammonia and extracted (4) with benzole, and, if salicin is to be sought, it is lastly extracted (5) with amylic alcohol.

Good beer, not sophisticated, when examined as directed above, gives the following results: The petroleum naphtha extract (1) contains (**a**) an amorphous, slightly bitter substance, soluble in ether and alcohol, and partially soluble in water; (**b**) a substance which precipitates basic acetate of lead; (**c**) a substance which becomes red with Fröhde's reagent;* and (**d**) one which becomes red with sulphuric acid and sugar. The benzole extract (2) contains the same substances and is more bitter; in addition it contains (**e**) a body which becomes dark brown when treated with sulphuric acid, and (**f**) a substance

given above is taken from that of C. R. A. Wright in **Journal of the Chemical Society,** 1874, 818.

* Fröhde's reagent is prepared by dissolving 0.01 gramme of sodium molybdate in 10 cub. cent. of concentrated sulphuric acid.

which precipitates tannic acid. The chloroform extract (3) contains substances **a**, **b**, **e**, and **f**; also (**g**) traces of a body precipitable by potassium iodide and phosphomolybdic acid; (**h**) a body which reduces ammoniacal silver nitrate; and (**i**) a body which crystallizes from ether and is difficultly soluble in alcohol. Of these substances, **b**, **c**, and **f** come from the hops; **a** from hops and malt together; **d**, **e**, **g**, and **h** from the malt; and **i** is formed from malt in fermentation.

In examination for foreign bitters which are not precipitable by basic lead acetate, it is better first to remove those natural constituents of beer which are precipitated by this re-agent, as follows:

II. 600 to 1000 c. c. are heated for removal of the carbonic acid; when cold, treated with basic lead acetate to completion of the precipitate; set aside some hours and then filtered. The lead is removed from the filtrate by adding excess of dilute sulphuric acid and filtering. The last filtrate is nearly or quite neutralized with ammonia, and evaporated, as quickly as possible, on the water-bath, to the volume of 180 to 200 c. c. If the filtrate has a harsh or bitter taste, the beer is to be suspected. The concentrated filtrate is now treated with petroleum naphtha, benzole, and the other solvents used in I., as directed for that method.

Normal beer, treated as directed in II., should give little or no extract with petroleum naphtha; but little benzole extract and that not bitter and not precipitating gold chloride, even on warming; and should give but a slight chloroform extract.

Of the EXTRACTS FROM THE ACID LIQUOR,—(1) **the residue from petroleum** may contain :—

Amorphous; with sulphuric acid, becoming first brown, then violet, and then red-violet . . **traces of Absinthin.**

Amorphous, colorless, sharp-tasting and rubefacient; with sulphuric acid, brown-red . . . **traces of Capsicin.**

Amorphous, green; with sulphuric acid and sugar becomes red; with ammoniacal silver solution gives no precipitate . . . . **Juniper-berry resin.**

Crystalline, yellow; with potassium cyanide becomes blood-red . . . . **Picric acid.**

(2) **The residue from benzole** may contain:

(A) Crystalline, not bitter; with potassa becoming purple-red; with sulphuric acid, red to orange. **Aloetin.**

(B) Amorphous.

(A) Gold chloride causes no precipitate in the water solution of the residue.

(a) Tannic acid gives no precipitate.

Sulphuric acid colors red-brown . . . **Capsicin.**

Sulphuric acid colors brown . . **Daphne bitter.**

(b) Tannic acid gives a precipitate. Residue bitter.

(aa) Basic acetate of lead causes a slight turbidity; sulphuric acid and sugar hardly redden.

Ferric chloride gives brown-green on warming the aqueous solution . . . **Gentian leaves.**

Ferric chloride gives a brown tint on warming; excessively bitter . . . . . . **Quassin.**

(bb) Basic acetate of lead gives a copious precipitate.

Sulphuric acid and sugar quickly give a cherry-red tint. Slightly bitter . . . . . **Cnicin.**

(B) Gold chloride does not precipitate the water solution of the residue in the cold, but is reduced on warming.

Tannic acid causes a slight precipitate; ammoniacal silver nitrate not reduced; dilute sulphuric acid with heat gives the odor of ericinol (characteristic, disagreeable); Fröhde's reagent gives a black-brown, and sulphuric acid and sugar a beautiful red color. . . . **Ledum bitter.**

Tannic acid precipitates; ammoniacal silver solution is reduced; hot sulphuric acid gives a slight odor of menyanthol . **Trifolium bitter.**

(c) Gold chloride precipitates the water solution of the residue in the cold, but does not reduce it on heating.

Sulphuric acid diluted with an equal weight of water gives a slight odor of benzoic acid . . **Centaury bitter.**

(d) Gold chloride precipitates the water solution in the cold, and is reduced on warming.

Sulphuric acid dissolves the residue to a brown tint at first soon turning violet, and becoming a beautiful violet on addition of water; hydrochloric acid of specific gravity 1.135, colors first green, then fine blue . **Absinthin.**

(3) **The residue from chloroform** may contain:

(A) Gold chloride giving no precipitate or reduction—

(a) Tannic acid giving no precipitate.

Sharp taste; epispastic; sulphuric acid colors dark brown-red . . . . **Capsicin.**

(b) Tannic acid precipitates.

(a) Basic lead acetate gives a considerable precipitate; dilute sulphuric acid with heat makes turbid, then brown-red, and gives a faint odor of benzoic acid . . . . **Cnicin.**

(b) Basic lead acetate gives little or no precipitate.
Sulphuric acid gives a brown color.
Residue very bitter . . . . **Quassin.**
Residue bitterish . . . . **Gentian.**
Residue sharp-tasting . . . **Daphne bitter.**
Sulphuric acid gives a slight yellow tint or no color at all . . . . **Colocynth.**

(B) Gold chloride gives no precipitate in the cold, but is reduced on warming.

(A) Tannic acid does not precipitate.
Stupefies fish; bitter taste . . . **Picrotoxin.**
Tasteless or slightly bitter; potassa colors red-brown . . . . **Aloes.**

(B) Tannic acid precipitates.
Ammoniacal silver nitrate reduced; sulphuric acid with heat gives a strong odor of menyanthol. **Menyanthin**
Ammoniacal silver not reduced; dilute sulphuric acid gives odor of ericinol; sulphuric acid and sugar, on standing, a carmine-red . . . . **Ledum bitter.** (ERICOLIN).

(C) Gold chloride precipitates in the cold, and is not reduced on warming.
Nitric acid gives a violet tint . . . **Colchicum.**
Sulphuric acid, with heat, gives odor of menyanthol; the liquid then turns red, and the odor alters to one resembling benzoic acid . . . **Centuary bitter.**

(D) Gold chloride precipitates in the cold, and reduces on heating.
Sulphuric acid colors brown to violet. [See (2), (B), (D)] . . . . **Wormwood bitter.**

OF THE EXTRACTS OF THE ALKALINE LIQUOR,—

(4) **The residue from benzole** may contain,—

(A) Dilating the pupils of a cat's eye,—

(a) Platinic chloride does not precipitate the aqueous solution:
Sulphuric acid, with heat, gives a peculiar odor. **Atropia.**

(b) Platinic chloride precipitates when in just the right proportion . . . . . . **Hyoscyamia.**

(B) Does not dilate the pupils of a cat's eye,—
Sulphuric acid solution, with potassium dichromate, becomes blue, soon fading . **Strychnia.**
Sulphuric acid solution becomes red with nitric acid . . . . **Brucia.**

TABLE OF REFERENCES,

TO SERVE AS

AN OUTLINE OF THE ORDER OF EXAMINATIONS.*

The figures refer to paragraphs.

"Alcohol" of commerce.

Constituents, commercial grades, strength,—12.
Identification of ethylic alcohol,—50.
Examination for **Fusel-oil**,—57 to 61.
for Acetic acid,—64 to 70.
for Aldehyde,—71.
for Methylic alcohol,—62.
(for Ether,—79).
Determination of alcohol,—51 to 56.

Whiskey.

Constituents,—14, 15, 16.
Adulterations,—16.
Determination of alcohol,—51 to 56.
Examination for **Fusel-oil**,—59 to 61, (57 and 58).
for Creosote,—77.
for Aromatics,—101½.
(for Bitters,—103).
for **Color**,—98, 99, 100.
(for Astringents,—86, 87).

* In this table it is only attempted to index the more prominent analytical points, giving references which lead to other suggestions for analysis in the body of the work.

INDEX.

SCIENTIFIC BOOKS

PUBLISHED BY

D. VAN NOSTRAND,

23 MURRAY STREET & 27 WARREN STREET,

NEW YORK.

Weisbach's Mechanics.

New and Revised Edition.

8vo. Cloth. $10.00.

A MANUAL OF THE MECHANICS OF ENGINEERING, and of the Construction of Machines. By JULIUS WEISBACH, PH. D. Translated from the fourth augmented and improved German edition, by ECKLEY B. COXE, A.M., Mining Engineer. Vol. I.—Theoretical Mechanics. 1,100 pages, and 902 wood-cut illustrations.

ABSTRACT OF CONTENTS.—Introduction to the Calculus—The General Principles of Mechanics—Phoronomics, or the Purely Mathematical Theory of Motion—Mechanics, or the General Physical Theory of Motion—Statics of Rigid Bodies—The Application of Statics to Elasticity and Strength—Dynamics of Rigid Bodies—Statics of Fluids—Dynamics of Fluids—The Theory of Oscillation, etc.

"The present edition is an entirely new work, greatly extended and very much improved. It forms a text-book which must find its way into the hands, not only of every student, but of every engineer who desires to refresh his memory or acquire clear ideas on doubtful points."—*Manufacturer and Builder.*

"We hope the day is not far distant when a thorough course of study and education as such shall be demanded of the practising engineer, and with this view we are glad to welcome this translation to our tongue and shores of one of the most able of the educators of Europe."—*The Technologist.*

Francis' Lowell Hydraulics.

Third Edition.

4to. Cloth. $15.00.

LOWELL HYDRAULIC EXPERIMENTS — being a Selection from Experiments on Hydraulic Motors, on the Flow of Water over Weirs, and in Open Canals of Uniform Rectangular Section, made at Lowell, Mass. By J. B. FRANCIS, Civil Engineer. Third edition, revised and enlarged, including many New Experiments on Gauging Water in Open Canals, and on the Flow through Submerged Orifices and Diverging Tubes. With 23 copperplates, beautifully engraved, and about 100 new pages of text.

The work is divided into parts. PART I., on hydraulic motors, includes ninety-two experiments on an improved Fourneyron Turbine Water-Wheel, of about two hundred horse-power, with rules and tables for the construction of similar motors; thirteen experiments on a model of a centre-vent water-wheel of the most simple design, and thirty-nine experiments on a centre-vent water-wheel of about two hundred and thirty horse-power.

PART II. includes seventy-four experiments made for the purpose of determining the form of the formula for computing the flow of water over weirs; nine experiments on the effect of back-water on the flow over weirs; eighty-eight experiments made for the purpose of determining the formula for computing the flow over weirs of regular or standard forms, with several tables of comparisons of the new formula with the results obtained by former experimenters; five experiments on the flow over a dam in which the crest was of the same form as that built by the Essex Company across the Merrimack River at Lawrence, Massachusetts; twenty-one experiments on the effect of observing the depths of water on a weir at different distances from the weir; an extensive series of experiments made for the purpose of determining rules for gauging streams of water in open canals, with tables for facilitating the same; and one hundred and one experiments on the discharge of water through submerged orifices and diverging tubes, the whole being fully illustrated by twenty-three double plates engraved on copper.

In 1855 the proprietors of the Locks and Canals on Merrimack River consented to the publication of the first edition of this work, which contained a selection of the most important hydraulic experiments made at Lowell up to that time. In this edition the principal hydraulic experiments made there, subsequent to 1855, have been added, including the important series above mentioned, for determining rules for the gauging the flow of water in open canals, and the interesting series on the flow through a submerged Venturi's tube, in which a larger flow was obtained than any we find recorded.

Francis on Cast-Iron Pillars.

8vo. Cloth. $2.00.

ON THE STRENGTH OF CAST-IRON PILLARS, with Tables for the use of Engineers, Architects, and Builders. By JAMES B. FRANCIS, Civil Engineer.

Merrill's Iron Truss Bridges.

Second Edition.

4to. Cloth. $5.00.

IRON TRUSS BRIDGES FOR RAILROADS. The Method of Calculating Strains in Trusses, with a careful comparison of the most prominent Trusses, in reference to economy in combination, etc., etc. By Brevet Colonel WILLIAM E. MERRILL, U.S.A., Major Corps of Engineers. Nine lithographed plates of illustrations.

"The work before us is an attempt to give a basis for sound reform in this feature of railroad engineering, by throwing 'additional light upon the method of calculating the maxima strains that can come upon any part of a bridge truss, and upon the manner of proportioning each part, so that it shall be as strong relatively to its own strains as any other part, and so that the entire bridge may be strong enough to sustain several times as great strains as the greatest that can come upon it in actual use.'"—*Scientific American.*

"The author has presented his views in a clear and intelligent manner, and the ingenuity displayed in coloring the figures so as to present certain facts to the eye forms no inappreciable part of the merits of the work. The reduction of the 'formulæ for obtaining the strength, volume, and weight of a cast-iron pillar under a strain of compression,' will be very acceptable to those who have occasion hereafter to make investigations involving these conditions. As a whole, the work has been well done."—*Railroad Gazette, Chicago.*

Humber's Strains in Girders.

18mo. Cloth. $2.50.

A HANDY BOOK FOR THE CALCULATION OF STRAINS IN GIRDERS and Similar Structures, and their Strength, consisting of Formulæ and Corresponding Diagrams, with numerous details for practical application. By WILLIAM HUMBER. Fully illustrated.

Shreve on Bridges and Roofs.

8vo, 87 wood-cut illustrations. Cloth. $5.00.

A TREATISE ON THE STRENGTH OF BRIDGES AND ROOFS—comprising the determination of Algebraic formulas for Strains in Horizontal, Inclined or Rafter, Triangular, Bowstring, Lenticular and other Trusses, from fixed and moving loads, with practical applications and examples, for the use of Students and Engineers. By SAMUEL H. SHREVE, A.M., Civil Engineer.

"On the whole, Mr. Shreve has produced a book which is the simplest, clearest, and at the same time, the most systematic and with the best mathematical reasoning of any work upon the same subject in the language."—*Railroad Gazette.*

"From the unusually clear language in which Mr. Shreve has given every statement, the student will have but himself to blame if he does not become thorough master of the subject."—*London Mining Journal.*

"Mr. Shreve has produced a work that must always take high rank as a text-book, * * * and no Bridge Engineer should be without it, as a valuable work of reference, and one that will frequently assist him out of difficulties."—*Franklin Institute Journal.*

The Kansas City Bridge.

4to. Cloth. $6.00

WITH AN ACCOUNT OF THE REGIMEN OF THE MISSOURI RIVER, and a description of the Methods used for Founding in that River. By O. CHANUTE, Chief Engineer, and GEORGE MORISON, Assistant Engineer. Illustrated with five lithographic views and twelve plates of plans.

Illustrations.

VIEWS.—View of the Kansas City Bridge, August 2, 1869. Lowering Caisson No. 1 into position. Caisson for Pier No. 4 brought into position. View of Foundation Works, Pier No. 4. Pier No. 1.

PLATES.—I. Map showing location of Bridge. II. Water Record—Cross Section of River—Profile of Crossing—Pontoon Protection. III. Water Deadener—Caisson No. 2—Foundation Works, Pier No. 3. IV. Foundation Works, Pier No. 4. V. Foundation Works, Pier No. 4. VI. Caisson No. 5—Sheet Piling at Pier No. 6—Details of Dredges—Pile Shoe—Beton Box. VII. Masonry—Draw Protection—False Works between Piers 3 and 4. VIII. Floating Derricks. IX. General Elevation—176 feet span. X. 248 feet span. XI. Plans of Draw. XII. Strain Diagrams.

Clarke's Quincy Bridge.

4to. Cloth. $7.50.

DESCRIPTION OF THE IRON RAILWAY Bridge across the Mississippi River at Quincy, Illinois. By THOMAS CURTIS CLARKE, Chief Engineer. Illustrated with twenty-one lithographed plans.

Illustrations.

PLATES.—General Plan of Mississippi River at Quincy, showing location of Bridge. II*a*. General Sections of Mississippi River at Quincy, showing location of Bridge. II*b*. General Sections of Mississippi River at Quincy, showing location of Bridge. III. General Sections of Mississippi River at Quincy, showing location of Bridge. IV. Plans of Masonry. V. Diagram of Spans, showing the Dimensions, Arrangement of Panels, etc. VI. Two hundred and fifty feet span, and details. VII. Three hundred and sixty feet Pivot Draw. VIII. Details of three hundred and sixty feet Draw. IX. Ice-Breakers, Foundations of Piers and Abutments, Water Table, and Curve of Deflections. X. Foundations of Pier 2, in Process of Construction. XI. Foundations of Pier 3, and its Protection. XII. Foundations of Pier 3, in Process of Construction, and Steam Dredge. XIII. Foundations of Piers 5 to 18, in Process of Construction. XIV. False Works, showing Process of Handling and Setting Stone. XV. False Works for Raising Iron Work of Superstructure. XVI. Steam Dredge used in Foundations 9 to 18. XVII. Single Bucket Dredge used in Foundations of Bay Piers. XVIII. Saws used for Cutting Piles under water. XIX. Sand Pump and Concrete Box. XX. Masonry Travelling Crane.

Whipple on Bridge Building.

8vo, Illustrated. Cloth. $4.00.

AN ELEMENTARY AND PRACTICAL TREATISE ON BRIDGE BUILDING. An enlarged and improved edition of the Author's original work. By S. WHIPPLE, C. E., Inventor of the Whipple Bridges, &c. Second Edition.

The design has been to develop from Fundamental Principles a system easy of comprehension, and such as to enable the attentive reader and student to judge understandingly for himself, as to the relative merits of different plans and combinations, and to adopt for use such as may be most suitable for the cases he may have to deal with.

It is hoped the work may prove an appropriate Text-Book upon the subject treated of, for the Engineering Student, and a useful manual for the Practicing Engineer and Bridge Builder.

Stoney on Strains.

New and Revised Edition, with numerous illustrations.

Royal 8vo, 664 pp. Cloth. $12.50.

THE THEORY OF STRAINS IN GIRDERS and Similar Structures, with Observations on the Application of Theory to Practice, and Tables of Strength and other Properties of Materials. By BINDON B. STONEY, B. A.

Roebling's Bridges.

Imperial folio. Cloth. $25.00.

LONG AND SHORT SPAN RAILWAY BRIDGES. By JOHN A. ROEBLING, C. E. Illustrated with large copperplate engravings of plans and views.

List of Plates

1. Parabolic Truss Railway Bridge. 2, 3, 4, 5, 6. Details of Parabolic Truss, with centre span 500 feet in the clear. 7. Plan and View of a Bridge over the Mississippi River, at St. Louis, for railway and common travel. 8, 9, 10, 11, 12. Details and View of St. Louis Bridge. 13. Railroad Bridge over the Ohio.

Diedrichs' Theory of Strains.

8vo. Cloth. $5.00.

A Compendium for the Calculation and Construction of Bridges, Roofs, and Cranes, with the Application of Trigonometrical Notes. Containing the most comprehensive information in regard to the Resulting Strains for a permanent Load, as also for a combined (Permanent and Rolling) Load. In two sections adapted to the requirements of the present time. By JOHN DIEDRICHS. Illustrated by numerous plates and diagrams.

"The want of a compact, universal and popular treatise on the Construction of Roofs and Bridges—especially one treating of the influence of a variable load—and the unsatisfactory essays of different authors on the subject, induced me to prepare this work."

Whilden's Strength of Materials.

12mo. Cloth. $2.00.

ON THE STRENGTH OF MATERIALS used in Engineering Construction. By J. K. Whilden.

Campin on Iron Roofs.

Large 8vo. Cloth. $2.00.

ON THE CONSTRUCTION OF IRON ROOFS. A Theoretical and Practical Treatise. By Francis Campin. With wood-cuts and plates of Roofs lately executed.

"The mathematical formulas are of an elementary kind, and the process admits of an easy extension so as to embrace the prominent varieties of iron truss bridges. The treatise, though of a practical scientific character, may be easily mastered by any one familiar with elementary mechanics and plane trigonometry."

Holley's Railway Practice.

1 vol. folio. Cloth. $12.00.

AMERICAN AND EUROPEAN RAILWAY PRACTICE, in the Economical Generation of Steam, including the materials and construction of Coal-burning Boilers, Combustion, the Variable Blast, Vaporization, Circulation, Super-heating, Supplying and Heating Feed-water, &c., and the adaptation of Wood and Coke-burning Engines to Coal-burning; and in Permanent Way, including Road-bed, Sleepers, Rails, Joint Fastenings, Street Railways, &c., &c. By Alexander L. Holley, B. P. With 77 lithographed plates.

"This is an elaborate treatise by one of our ablest civil engineers, on the construction and use of locomotives, with a few chapters on the building of Railroads. * * * All these subjects are treated by the author, who is a first-class railroad engineer, in both an intelligent and intelligible manner. The facts and ideas are well arranged, and presented in a clear and simple style, accompanied by beautiful engravings, and we presume the work will be regarded as indispensable by all who are interested in a knowledge of the construction of railroads and rolling stock, or the working of locomotives."—*Scientific American.*

Henrici's Skeleton Structures.

8vo. Cloth. $1.50.

SKELETON STRUCTURES, especially in their Application to the building of Steel and Iron Bridges. By Olaus Henrici. With folding plates and diagrams.

By presenting these general examinations on Skeleton Structures, with particular application for Suspended Bridges, to Engineers, I venture to express the hope that they will receive these theoretical results with some confidence, even although an opportunity is wanting to compare them with practical results. O. H.

Useful Information for Railway Men.

Pocket form. Morocco, gilt, $2.00.

Compiled by W. G. Hamilton, Engineer. Fifth edition, revised and enlarged. 570 pages.

"It embodies many valuable formulæ and recipes useful for railway men, and, indeed, for almost every class of persons in the world. The 'information' comprises some valuable formulæ and rules for the construction of boilers and engines, masonry, properties of steel and iron, and the strength of materials generally."—*Railroad Gazette, Chicago.*

Brooklyn Water Works.

1 vol. folio. Cloth. $25.00.

A DESCRIPTIVE ACCOUNT OF THE CONSTRUCTION OF THE WORKS, and also Reports on the Brooklyn, Hartford, Belleville, and Cambridge Pumping Engines. Prepared and printed by order of the Board of Water Commissioners. With 59 illustrations.

Contents.—Supply Ponds—The Conduit—Ridgewood Engine House and Pump Well—Ridgewood Engines—Force Mains—Ridgewood Reservoir—Pipe Distribution—Mount Prospect Reservoir—Mount Prospect Engine House and Engine—Drainage Grounds—Sewerage Works—Appendix.

Kirkwood on Filtration.

4to. Cloth. $15.00.

REPORT ON THE FILTRATION OF RIVER WATERS, for the Supply of Cities, as practised in Europe, made to the Board of Water Commissioners of the City of St. Louis. By JAMES P. KIRKWOOD. Illustrated by 30 double-plate engravings.

CONTENTS.—Report on Filtration—London Works, General—Chelsea Water Works and Filters—Lambeth Water Works and Filters—Southwark and Vauxhall Water Works and Filters—Grand Junction Water Works and Filters—West Middlesex Water Works and Filters—New River Water Works and Filters—East London Water Works and Filters—Leicester Water Works and Filters—York Water Works and Filters—Liverpool Water Works and Filters—Edinburgh Water Works and Filters—Dublin Water Works and Filters—Perth Water Works and Filtering Gallery—Berlin Water Works and Filters—Hamburg Water Works and Reservoirs—Altona Water Works and Filters—Tours Water Works and Filtering Canal—Angers Water Works and Filtering Galleries—Nantes Water Works and Filters—Lyons Water Works and Filtering Galleries—Toulouse Water Works and Filtering Galleries—Marseilles Water Works and Filters—Genoa Water Works and Filtering Galleries—Leghorn Water Works and Cisterns—Wakefield Water Works and Filters—Appendix.

Tunner on Roll-Turning.

1 vol. 8vo. and 1 vol. plates. $10.00.

A TREATISE ON ROLL-TURNING FOR THE MANUFACTURE OF IRON. By PETER TUNNER. Translated and adapted. By JOHN B. PEARSE, of the Pennsylvania Steel Works. With numerous wood-cuts, 8vo., together with a folio atlas of 10 lithographed plates of Rolls, Measurements, &c.

"We commend this book as a clear, elaborate, and practical treatise upon the department of iron manufacturing operations to which it is devoted. The writer states in his preface, that for twenty-five years he has felt the necessity of such a work, and has evidently brought to its preparation the fruits of experience, a painstaking regard for accuracy of statement, and a desire to furnish information in a style readily understood. The book should be in the hands of every one interested, either in the general practice of mechanical engineering, or the special branch of manufacturing operations to which the work relates."—*American Artisan.*

Glynn on the Power of Water.

12mo. Cloth. $1.00.

A TREATISE ON THE POWER OF WATER, as applied to drive Flour Mills, and to give motion to Turbines and other Hydrostatic Engines. By JOSEPH GLYNN, F.R. S. Third edition, revised and enlarged, with numerous illustrations.

Hewson on Embankments.

8vo. Cloth. $2.00.

PRINCIPLES AND PRACTICE OF EMBANKING LANDS from River Floods, as applied to the Levees of the Mississippi. By WILLIAM HEWSON, Civil Engineer.

"This is a valuable treatise on the principles and practice of embanking lands from river floods, as applied to the Levees of the Mississippi, by a highly intelligent and experienced engineer. The author says it is a first attempt to reduce to order and to rule the design, execution, and measurement of the Levees of the Mississippi. It is a most useful and needed contribution to scientific literature.—*Philadelphia Evening Journal.*

Grüner on Steel.

8vo. Cloth. $3.50.

THE MANUFACTURE OF STEEL. By M. L. GRUNER, translated from the French. By Lenox Smith, A. M., E. M., with an appendix on the Bessemer Process in the United States, by the translator. Illustrated by lithographed drawings and wood-cuts.

"The purpose of the work is to present a careful, elaborate, and at the same time practical examination into the physical properties of steel, as well as a description of the new processes and mechanical appliances for its manufacture. The information which it contains, gathered from many trustworthy sources, will be found of much value to the American steel manufacturer, who may thus acquaint himself with the results of careful and elaborate experiments in other countries, and better prepare himself for successful competition in this important industry with foreign makers. The fact that this volume is from the pen of one of the ablest metallurgists of the present day, cannot fail, we think, to secure for it a favorable consideration.—*Iron Age.*

Bauerman on Iron.

12mo. Cloth. $2.00.

TREATISE ON THE METALLURGY OF IRON. Containing outlines of the History of Iron Manufacture, methods of Assay, and analysis of Iron Ores, processes of manufacture of Iron and Steel, etc., etc. By H. BAUERMAN. First American edition. Revised and enlarged, with an appendix on the Martin Process for making Steel, from the report of Abram S. Hewitt. Illustrated with numerous wood engravings.

"This is an important addition to the stock of technical works published in this country. It embodies the latest facts, discoveries, and processes connected with the manufacture of iron and steel, and should be in the hands of every person interested in the subject, as well as in all technical and scientific libraries."—*Scientific American.*

Link and Valve Motions, by W. S. Auchincloss.

8vo. Cloth. $3.00.

APPLICATION OF THE SLIDE VALVE and Link Motion to Stationary, Portable, Locomotive and Marine Engines, with new and simple methods for proportioning the parts. By WILLIAM S. AUCHINCLOSS, Civil and Mechanical Engineer. Designed as a hand-book for Mechanical Engineers, Master Mechanics, Draughtsmen and Students of Steam Engineering. All dimensions of the valve are found with the greatest ease by means of a Printed Scale, and proportions of the link determined *without* the assistance of a model. Illustrated by 37 wood-cuts and 21 lithographic plates, together with a copperplate engraving of the Travel Scale.

All the matters we have mentioned are treated with a clearness and absence of unnecessary verbiage which renders the work a peculiarly valuable one. The Travel Scale only requires to be known to be appreciated. Mr. A. writes so ably on his subject, we wish he had written more. *London Engineering.*

We have never opened a work relating to steam which seemed to us better calculated to give an intelligent mind a clear understanding of the department it discusses.—*Scientific American.*

Slide Valve by Eccentrics, by Prof. C. W. MacCord.

4to. Illustrated. Cloth, $4.00.

A PRACTICAL TREATISE ON THE SLIDE VALVE BY ECCENTRICS, examining by methods, the action of the Eccentric upon the Slide Valve, and explaining the practical processes of laying out the movements, adapting the valve for its various duties in the steam-engine. For the use of Engineers, Draughtsmen, Machinists, and Students of valve motions in general. By C. W. MacCord, A. M., Professor of Mechanical Drawing, Stevens' Institute of Technology, Hoboken, N. J.

Stillman's Steam-Engine Indicator.

12mo. Cloth. $1.00.

THE STEAM-ENGINE INDICATOR, and the Improved Manometer Steam and Vacuum Gauges; their utility and application By Paul Stillman. New edition.

Bacon's Steam-Engine Indicator.

12mo. Cloth. $1.00. Mor. $1.50.

A TREATISE ON THE RICHARDS STEAM-ENGINE INDICATOR, with directions for its use. By Charles T. Porter. Revised, with notes and large additions as developed by American Practice, with an Appendix containing useful formulæ and rules for Engineers. By F. W. Bacon, M. E., Member of the American Society of Civil Engineers. Illustrated. Second Edition

In this work, Mr. Porter's book has been taken as the basis, but Mr. Bacon has adapted it to American Practice, and has conferred a great boon on American Engineers.—*Artisan.*

Bartol on Marine Boilers.

8vo. Cloth. $1.50.

TREATISE ON THE MARINE BOILERS OF THE UNITED STATES. By H. B. Bartol. Illustrated.

Gillmore's Limes and Cements.

Fourth Edition. Revised and Enlargd.

8vo. Cloth. $4.00.

PRACTICAL TREATISE ON LIMES, HYDRAULIC CEMENTS, AND MORTARS. Papers on Practical Engineering, U. S. Engineer Department, No. 9, containing Reports of numerous experiments conducted in New York City, during the years 1858 to 1861, inclusive. By Q. A. GILLMORE, Brig-General U. S. Volunteers, and Major U. S. Corps of Engineers. With numerous illustrations.

"This work contains a record of certain experiments and researches made under the authority of the Engineer Bureau of the War Department from 1858 to 1861, upon the various hydraulic cements of the United States, and the materials for their manufacture. The experiments were carefully made, and are well reported and compiled."—*Journal Franklin Institute.*

Gillmore's Coignet Beton.

8vo. Cloth. $2.50.

COIGNET BETON AND OTHER ARTIFICIAL STONE. By Q. A. GILLMORE. 9 Plates, Views, etc.

This work describes with considerable minuteness of detail the several kinds of artificial stone in most general use in Europe and now beginning to be introduced in the United States, discusses their properties, relative merits, and cost, and describes the materials of which they are composed. . . . . The subject is one of special and growing interest, and we commend the work, embodying as it does the matured opinions of an experienced engineer and expert.

Williamson's Practical Tables.

4to. Flexible Cloth. $2.50.

PRACTICAL TABLES IN METEOROLOGY AND HYPSOMETRY, in connection with the use of the Barometer. By Col. R. S. WILLIAMSOM, U. S. A.

Williamson on the Barometer.

4to. Cloth. $15.00.

ON THE USE OF THE BAROMETER ON SURVEYS AND RECONNAISSANCES. Part I. Meteorology in its Connection with Hypsometry. Part II. Barometric Hypsometry. By R. S. WILLIAMSON, Bvt. Lieut.-Col. U. S. A., Major Corps of Engineers. With Illustrative Tables and Engravings. Paper No. 15, Professional Papers, Corps of Engineers.

"SAN FRANCISCO, CAL., *Feb.* 27, 1867.

"Gen. A. A. HUMPHREYS, Chief of Engineers, U. S. Army:

"GENERAL,—I have the honor to submit to you, in the following pages, the results of my investigations in meteorology and hypsometry, made with the view of ascertaining how far the barometer can be used as a reliable instrument for determining altitudes on extended lines of survey and reconnaissances. These investigations have occupied the leisure permitted me from my professional duties during the last ten years, and I hope the results will be deemed of sufficient value to have a place assigned them among the printed professional papers of the United States Corps of Engineers.

"Very respectfully, your obedient servant,

"R. S. WILLIAMSON,

"Bvt. Lt.-Col. U. S. A., Major Corps of U. S. Engineers."

Von Cotta's Ore Deposits.

8vo. Cloth. $4.00.

TREATISE ON ORE DEPOSITS. By BERNHARD VON COTTA, Professor of Geology in the Royal School of Mines, Freidberg, Saxony. Translated from the second German edition, by FREDERICK PRIME, Jr., Mining Engineer, and revised by the author, with numerous illustrations.

"Prof. Von Cotta of the Freiberg School of Mines, is the author of the best modern treatise on ore deposits, and we are heartily glad that this admirable work has been translated and published in this country. The translator, Mr. Frederick Prime, Jr., a graduate of Freiberg, has had in his work the great advantage of a revision by the author himself, who declares in a prefatory note that this may be considered as a new edition (the third) of his own book.

"It is a timely and welcome contribution to the literature of mining in this country, and we are grateful to the translator for his enterprise and good judgment in undertaking its preparation; while we recognize with equal cordiality the liberality of the author in granting both permission and assistance."—*Extract from Review in Engineering and Mining Journal.*

Plattner's Blow-Pipe Analysis.

Second edition. Revised. 8vo. Cloth. $7.50.

PLATTNER'S MANUAL OF QUALITATIVE AND QUANTITATIVE ANALYSIS WITH THE BLOW-PIPE. From the last German edition Revised and enlarged. By Prof. TH. RICHTER, of the Royal Saxon Mining Academy. Translated by Prof. H. B. CORNWALL, Assistant in the Columbia School of Mines, New York; assisted by JOHN H. CASWELL. Illustrated with eighty-seven wood-cuts and one Lithographic Plate. 560 pages.

"Plattner's celebrated work has long been recognized as the only complete book on Blow-Pipe Analysis. The fourth German edition, edited by Prof. Richter, fully sustains the reputation which the earlier editions acquired during the lifetime of the author, and it is a source of great satisfaction to us to know that Prof. Richter has co-operated with the translator in issuing the American edition of the work, which is in fact a fifth edition of the original work, being far more complete than the last German edition."—*Silliman's Journal.*

There is nothing so complete to be found in the English language. Plattner's book is not a mere pocket edition; it is intended as a comprehensive guide to all that is at present known on the blow-pipe, and as such is really indispensable to teachers and advanced pupils.

"Mr. Cornwall's edition is something more than a translation, as it contains many corrections, emendations and additions not to be found in the original. It is a decided improvement on the work in its German dress."—*Journal of Applied Chemistry.*

Egleston's Mineralogy.

8vo. Illustrated with 34 Lithographic Plates. Cloth. $4.50.

LECTURES ON DESCRIPTIVE MINERALOGY, Delivered at the School of Mines, Columbia College. BY PROFESSOR T. EGLESTON.

These lectures are what their title indicates, the lectures on Mineralogy delivered at the School of Mines of Columbia College. They have been printed for the students, in order that more time might be given to the various methods of examining and determining minerals. The second part has only been printed. The first part, comprising crystallography and physical mineralogy, will be printed at some future time.

Pynchon's Chemical Physics.

New Edition. Revised and Enlarged.

Crown 8vo. Cloth. $3.00.

INTRODUCTION TO CHEMICAL PHYSICS, Designed for the Use of Academies, Colleges, and High Schools. Illustrated with numerous engravings, and containing copious experiments with directions for preparing them. By THOMAS RUGGLES PYNCHON, M.A., Professor of Chemistry and the Natural Sciences, Trinity College, Hartford.

Hitherto, no work suitable for general use, treating of all these subjects within the limits of a single volume, could be found; consequently the attention they have received has not been at all proportionate to their importance. It is believed that a book containing so much valuable information within so small a compass, cannot fail to meet with a ready sale among all intelligent persons, while Professional men, Physicians, Medical Students, Photographers, Telegraphers, Engineers, and Artisans generally, will find it specially valuable, if not nearly indispensable, as a book of reference.

"We strongly recommend this able treatise to our readers as the first work ever published on the subject free from perplexing technicalities. In style it is pure, in description graphic, and its typographical appearance is artistic. It is altogether a most excellent work."—*Eclectic Medical Journal.*

"It treats fully of Photography, Telegraphy, Steam Engines, and the various applications of Electricity. In short, it is a carefully prepared volume, abreast with the latest scientific discoveries and inventions."—*Hartford Courant.*

Plympton's Blow-Pipe Analysis.

12mo. Cloth. $1 50.

THE BLOW-PIPE: A Guide to Its Use in the Determination of Salts and Minerals. Compiled from various sources, by GEORGE W. PLYMPTON, C.E., A.M., Professor of Physical Science in the Polytechnic Institute, Brooklyn, N. Y.

"This manual probably has no superior in the English language as a text-book for beginners, or as a guide to the student working without a teacher. To the latter many illustrations of the utensils and apparatus required in using the blow-pipe, as well as the fully illustrated description of the blow-pipe flame, will be especially serviceable."—*New York Teacher.*

Ure's Dictionary.

Sixth Edition.

London, 1872.

3 vols. 8vo. Cloth, $25.00. Half Russia, $32.50.

DICTIONARY OF ARTS, MANUFACTURES, AND MINES. By ANDREW URE, M.D. Sixth edition. Edited by ROBERT HUNT, F.R.S., greatly enlarged and rewritten.

Brande and Cox's Dictionary.

New Edition.

London, 1872.

3 vols. 8vo. Cloth, $20.00. Half Morocco, $27.50.

A Dictionary of Science, Literature, and Art. Edited by W. T. BRANDE and Rev. GEO. W. COX. New and enlarged edition.

Watt's Dictionary of Chemistry.

Supplementary Volume.

8vo. Cloth. $9.00.

This volume brings the Record of Chemical Discovery down to the end of the year 1869, including also several additions to, and corrections of, former results which have appeared in 1870 and 1871.

*** Complete Sets of the Work, New and Revised edition, including above supplement. 6 vols. 8vo. Cloth. $62.00.

Rammelsberg's Chemical Analysis.

8vo. Cloth. $2.25.

GUIDE TO A COURSE OF QUANTITATIVE CHEMICAL ANALYSIS, ESPECIALLY OF MINERALS AND FURNACE PRODUCTS. Illustrated by Examples. By C. F. RAMMELSBERG. Translated by J. TOWLER, M.D.

This work has been translated, and is now published expressly for those students in chemistry whose time and other studies in colleges do not permit them to enter upon the more elaborate and expensive treatises of Fresenius and others. It is the condensed labor of a master in chemistry and of a practical analyst.

Eliot and Storer's Qualitative Chemical Analysis.

New Edition, Revised.

12mo. Illustrated. Cloth. $1.50.

A COMPENDIOUS MANUAL OF QUALITATIVE CHEMICAL ANALYSIS. By CHARLES W. ELIOT and FRANK H. STORER. Revised with the Coöperation of the Authors, by WILLIAM RIPLEY NICHOLS, Professor of Chemistry in the Massachusetts Institute of Technology.

"This Manual has great merits as a practical introduction to the science and the art of which it treats. It contains enough of the theory and practice of qualitative analysis, "in the wet way," to bring out all the reasoning involved in the science, and to present clearly to the student the most approved methods of the art. It is specially adapted for exercises and experiments in the laboratory; and yet its classifications and manner of treatment are so systematic and logical throughout, as to adapt it in a high degree to that higher class of students generally who desire an accurate knowledge of the practical methods of arriving at scientific facts."—*Lutheran Observer.*

"We wish every academical class in the land could have the benefit of the fifty exercises of two hours each necessary to master this book. Chemistry would cease to be a mere matter of memory, and become a pleasant experimental and intellectual recreation. We heartily commend this little volume to the notice of those teachers who believe in using the sciences as means of mental discipline."—*College Courant.*

Craig's Decimal System.

Square 32mo. Limp. 50c.

WEIGHTS AND MEASURES. An Account of the Decimal System, with Tables of Conversion for Commercial and Scientific Uses. By B. F. CRAIG, M. D.

"The most lucid, accurate, and useful of all the hand-books on this subject that we have yet seen. It gives forty-seven tables of comparison between the English and French denominations of length, area, capacity, weight, and the Centigrade and Fahrenheit thermometers, with clear instructions how to use them; and to this practical portion, which helps to make the transition as easy as possible, is prefixed a scientific explanation of the errors in the metric system, and how they may be corrected in the laboratory."—*Nation.*

Nugent on Optics.

12mo. Cloth. $2.00

TREATISE ON OPTICS; or, Light and Sight, theoretically and practically treated; with the application to Fine Art and Industrial Pursuits. By E. Nugent. With one hundred and three illustrations.

"This book is of a practical rather than a theoretical kind, and is designed to afford accurate and complete information to all interested in applications of the science."—*Round Table.*

Barnard's Metric System.

8vo. Brown cloth. $3.00.

THE METRIC SYSTEM OF WEIGHTS AND MEASURES. An Address delivered before the Convocation of the University of the State of New York, at Albany, August, 1871. By Frederick A. P. Barnard, President of Columbia College, New York City. Second edition from the Revised edition printed for the Trustees of Columbia College. Tinted paper.

"It is the best summary of the arguments in favor of the metric weights and measures with which we are acquainted, not only because it contains in small space the leading facts of the case, but because it puts the advocacy of that system on the only tenable grounds, namely, the great convenience of a decimal notation of weight and measure as well as money, the value of international uniformity in the matter, and the fact that this metric system is adopted and in general use by the majority of civilized nations."—*The Nation.*

The Young Mechanic.

Illustrated. 12mo. Cloth. $1.75.

THE YOUNG MECHANIC. Containing directions for the use of all kinds of tools, and for the construction of steam engines and mechanical models, including the Art of Turning in Wood and Metal. By the author of "The Lathe and its Uses," etc. From the English edition, with corrections.

Harrison's Mechanic's Tool-Book.

12mo. Cloth. $1.50.

MECHANIC'S TOOL BOOK, with practical rules and suggestions, for the use of Machinists, Iron Workers, and others. By W. B. Harrison, Associate Editor of the "American Artisan." Illustrated with 44 engravings.

"This work is specially adapted to meet the wants of Machinists and workers in iron generally. It is made up of the work-day experience of an intelligent and ingenious mechanic, who had the faculty of adapting tools to various purposes. The practicability of his plans and suggestions are made apparent even to the unpractised eye by a series of well-executed wood engravings."—*Philadelphia Inquirer*.

Pope's Modern Practice of the Electric Telegraph.

Eighth Edition. 8vo. Cloth $2.00.

A Hand-book for Electricians and Operators. By Frank L. Pope. Seventh edition. Revised and enlarged, and fully illustrated.

Extract from Letter of Prof. Morse.

"I have had time only cursorily to examine its contents, but this examination has resulted in great gratification, especially at the fairness and unprejudiced tone of your whole work.

"Your illustrated diagrams are admirable and beautifully executed.

"I think all your instructions in the use of the telegraph apparatus judicious and correct, and I most cordially wish you success."

Extract from Letter of Prof. G. W. Hough, of the Dudley Observatory.

"There is no other work of this kind in the English language that contains in so small a compass so much practical information in the application of galvanic electricity to telegraphy. It should be in the hands of every one interested in telegraphy, or the use of Batteries for other purposes."

Morse's Telegraphic Apparatus.

Illustrated. 8vo. Cloth. $2.00.

EXAMINATION OF THE TELEGRAPHIC APPARATUS AND THE PROCESSES IN TELEGAPHY. By Samuel F. B. Morse, LL.D., United States Commissioner Paris Universal Exposition, 1867.

Sabine's History of the Telegraph.

12mo. Cloth. $1.25.

HISTORY AND PROGRESS OF THE ELECTRIC TELEGRAPH, with Descriptions of some of the Apparatus. By ROBERT SABINE, C. E. Second edition, with additions.

CONTENTS.—I. Early Observations of Electrical Phenomena. II. Telegraphs by Frictional Electricity. III. Telegraphs by Voltaic Electricity. IV. Telegraphs by Electro-Magnetism and Magneto-Electricity. V. Telegraphs now in use. VI. Overhead Lines. VII. Submarine Telegraph Lines. VIII. Underground Telegraphs. IX. Atmospheric Electricity.

Haskins' Galvanometer.

Pocket form. Illustrated. Morocco tucks. $2.00.

THE GALVANOMETER, AND ITS USES; a Manual for Electricians and Students. By C. H. HASKINS.

"We hope this excellent little work will meet with the sale its merits entitle it to. To every telegrapher who owns, or uses a Galvanometer, or ever expects to, it will be quite indispensable."—*The Telegrapher*.

Culley's Hand-Book of Telegraphy.

8vo. Cloth. $5.00.

A HAND-BOOK OF PRACTICAL TELEGRAPHY. By R. S. CULLEY, Engineer to the Electric and International Telegraph Company. Fifth edition, revised and enlarged.

Foster's Submarine Blasting.

4to. Cloth. $3.50.

SUBMARINE BLASTING in Boston Harbor, Massachusetts—Removal of Tower and Corwin Rocks. By JOHN G. FOSTER, Lieutenant-Colonel of Engineers, and Brevet Major-General, U. S. Army. Illustrated with seven plates.

LIST OF PLATES.—1. Sketch of the Narrows, Boston Harbor. 2. Townsend's Submarine Drilling Machine, and Working Vessel attending. 3. Submarine Drilling Machine employed. 4. Details of Drilling Machine employed. 5. Cartridges and Tamping used. 6. Fuses and Insulated Wires used. 7. Portable Friction Battery used.

Barnes' Submarine Warfare.

8vo. Cloth. $5.00.

SUBMARINE WARFARE, DEFENSIVE AND OFFENSIVE. Comprising a full and complete History of the Invention of the Torpedo, its employment in War and results of its use. Descriptions of the various forms of Torpedoes, Submarine Batteries and Torpedo Boats actually used in War. Methods of Ignition by Machinery, Contact Fuzes, and Electricity, and a full account of experiments made to determine the Explosive Force of Gunpowder under Water. Also a discussion of the Offensive Torpedo system, its effect upon Iron-Clad Ship systems, and influence upon Future Naval Wars. By Lieut.-Commander JOHN S. BARNES, U. S. N. With twenty lithographic plates and many wood-cuts.

"A book important to military men, and especially so to engineers and artillerists. It consists of an examination of the various offensive and defensive engines that have been contrived for submarine hostilities, including a discussion of the torpedo system, its effects upon iron-clad ship-systems, and its probable influence upon future naval wars. Plates of a valuable character accompany the treatise, which affords a useful history of the momentous subject it discusses. A great deal of useful information is collected in its pages, especially concerning the inventions of SCHOLL and VERDU, and of JONES' and HUNT'S batteries, as well as of other similar machines, and the use in submarine operations of gun-cotton and nitro-glycerine."—*N. Y. Times.*

Randall's Quartz Operator's Hand-Book.

12mo. Cloth. $2.00.

QUARTZ OPERATOR'S HAND-BOOK. By P. M. RANDALL. New edition, revised and enlarged. Fully illustrated.

The object of this work has been to present a clear and comprehensive exposition of mineral veins, and the means and modes chiefly employed for the mining and working of their ores—more especially those containing gold and silver.

Mitchell's Manual of Assaying.

8vo. Cloth. $10.00.

A MANUAL OF PRACTICAL ASSAYING. By John Mitchell. Third edition. Edited by William Crookes, F.R.S.

In this edition are incorporated all the late important discoveries in Assaying made in this country and abroad, and special care is devoted to the very important Volumetric and Colorimetric Assays, as well as to the Blow-Pipe Assays.

Benét's Chronoscope.

Second Edition.

Illustrated. 4to. Cloth. $3.00.

ELECTRO-BALLISTIC MACHINES, and the Schultz Chronoscope. By Lieutenant-Colonel S. V. Benét, Captain of Ordnance, U. S. Army.

Contents.—1. Ballistic Pendulum. 2. Gun Pendulum. 3. Use of Electricity. 4. Navez' Machine. 5. Vignotti's Machine, with Plates. 6. Benton's Electro-Ballistic Pendulum, with Plates. 7. Leur's Tro-Pendulum Machine 8. Schultz's Chronoscope, with two Plates.

Michaelis' Chronograph.

4to. Illustrated. Cloth. $3.00.

THE LE BOULENGÉ CHRONOGRAPH. With three lithographed folding plates of illustrations. By Brevet Captain O E. Michaelis, First Lieutenant Ordnance Corps, U. S. Army.

"The excellent monograph of Captain Michaelis enters minutely into the details of construction and management, and gives tables of the times of flight calculated upon a given fall of the chronometer for all distances. Captain Michaelis has done good service in presenting this work to his brother officers, describing, as it does, an instrument which bids fair to be in constant use in our future ballistic experiments."—*Army and Navy Journal*

Silversmith's Hand-Book.

Fourth Edition.

Illustrated. 12mo. Cloth. $3.00.

A PRACTICAL HAND-BOOK FOR MINERS, Metallurgists, and Assayers, comprising the most recent improvements in the disintegration, amalgamation, smelting, and parting of the Precious Ores, with a Comprehensive Digest of the Mining Laws. Greatly augmented, revised, and corrected. By JULIUS SILVERSMITH. Fourth edition. Profusely illustrated. 1 vol. 12mo. Cloth. $3.00.

One of the most important features of this work is that in which the metallurgy of the precious metals is treated of. In it the author has endeavored to embody all the processes for the reduction and manipulation of the precious ores heretofore successfully employed in Germany, England, Mexico, and the United States, together with such as have been more recently invented, and not yet fully tested—all of which are profusely illustrated and easy of comprehension.

Simms' Levelling.

8vo. Cloth. $2.50.

A TREATISE ON THE PRINCIPLES AND PRACTICE OF LEVELLING, showing its application to purposes of Railway Engineering and the Construction of Roads, &c. By FREDERICK W. SIMMS, C. E. From the fifth London edition, revised and corrected, with the addition of Mr. Law's Practical Examples for Setting Out Railway Curves. Illustrated with three lithographic plates and numerous wood-cuts.

"One of the most important text-books for the general surveyor, and there is scarcely a question connected with levelling for which a solution would be sought, but that would be satisfactorily answered by consulting this volume." —*Mining Journal.*

"The text-book on levelling in most of our engineering schools and colleges."—*Engineers.*

"The publishers have rendered a substantial service to the profession, especially to the younger members, by bringing out the present edition of Mr. Simms' useful work."—*Engineering.*

Stuart's Successful Engineer.

18mo. Boards. 50 cents.

HOW TO BECOME A SUCCESSFUL ENGINEER: Being Hints to Youths intending to adopt the Profession. By BERNARD STUART, Engineer. Sixth Edition.

"A valuable little book of sound, sensible advice to young men who wish to rise in the most important of the professions."—*Scientific American.*

Stuart's Naval Dry Docks.

Twenty-four engravings on steel.

Fourth Edition.

4to. Cloth. $6.00.

THE NAVAL DRY DOCKS OF THE UNITED STATES. By CHARLES B. STUART, Engineer in Chief of the United States Navy.

List of Illustrations.

Pumping Engine and Pumps—Plan of Dry Dock and Pump-Well—Sections of Dry Dock—Engine House—Iron Floating Gate—Details of Floating Gate—Iron Turning Gate—Plan of Turning Gate—Culvert Gate—Filling Culvert Gates—Engine Bed—Plate, Pumps, and Culvert—Engine House Roof—Floating Sectional Dock—Details of Section, and Plan of Turn-Tables—Plan of Basin and Marine Railways—Plan of Sliding Frame, and Elevation of Pumps—Hydraulic Cylinder—Plan of Gearing for Pumps and End Floats—Perspective View of Dock, Basin, and Railway—Plan of Basin of Portsmouth Dry Dock—Floating Balance Dock—Elevation of Trusses and the Machinery—Perspective View of Balance Dry Dock

Free Hand Drawing.

Profusely Illustrated. 18mo. Boards. 50 cents.

A GUIDE TO ORNAMENTAL, Figure, and Landscape Drawing. By an Art Student.

CONTENTS.—Materials employed in Drawing, and how to use them—On Lines and how to Draw them—On Shading—Concerning lines and shading, with applications of them to simple elementary subjects—Sketches from Nature.

Minifie's Mechanical Drawing.

Eighth Edition.

Royal 8vo. Cloth. $4.00.

A TEXT-BOOK OF GEOMETRICAL DRAWING for the use of Mechanics and Schools, in which the Definitions and Rules of Geometry are familiarly explained; the Practical Problems are arranged, from the most simple to the more complex, and in their description technicalities are avoided as much as possible. With illustrations for Drawing Plans, Sections, and Elevations of Buildings and Machinery; an Introduction to Isometrical Drawing, and an Essay on Linear Perspective and Shadows. Illustrated with over 200 diagrams engraved on steel. By WM. MINIFIE, Architect. Eighth Edition. With an Appendix on the Theory and Application of Colors.

"It is the best work on Drawing that we have ever seen, and is especially a text-book of Geometrical Drawing for the use of Mechanics and Schools. No young Mechanic, such as a Machinist, Engineer, Cabinet-Maker, Millwright, or Carpenter, should be without it."—*Scientific American.*

"One of the most comprehensive works of the kind ever published, and cannot but possess great value to builders. The style is at once elegant and substantial."—*Pennsylvania Inquirer.*

"Whatever is said is rendered perfectly intelligible by remarkably well-executed diagrams on steel, leaving nothing for mere vague supposition; and the addition of an introduction to isometrical drawing, linear perspective, and the projection of shadows, winding up with a useful index to technical terms." —*Glasgow Mechanics' Journal.*

☞ The British Government has authorized the use of this book in their schools of art at Somerset House, London, and throughout the kingdom.

Minifie's Geometrical Drawing.

New Edition. Enlarged.

12mo. Cloth. $2.00.

GEOMETRICAL DRAWING. Abridged from the octavo edition, for the use of Schools. Illustrated with 48 steel plates. New edition, enlarged.

"It is well adapted as a text-book of drawing to be used in our High Schools and Academies where this useful branch of the fine arts has been hitherto too much neglected."—*Boston Journal.*

Bell on Iron Smelting.

8vo. Cloth. $6.00.

CHEMICAL PHENOMENA OF IRON SMELTING. An experimental and practical examination of the circumstances which determine the capacity of the Blast Furnace, the Temperature of the Air, and the Proper Condition of the Materials to be operated upon. By I. LOWTHIAN BELL.

"The reactions which take place in every foot of the blast-furnace have been investigated, and the nature of every step in the process, from the introduction of the raw material into the furnace to the production of the pig iron, has been carefully ascertained, and recorded so fully that any one in the trade can readily avail themselves of the knowledge acquired; and we have no hesitation in saying that the judicious application of such knowledge will do much to facilitate the introduction of arrangements which will still further economize fuel, and at the same time permit of the quality of the resulting metal being maintained, if not improved. The volume is one which no practical pig iron manufacturer can afford to be without if he be desirous of entering upon that competition which nowadays is essential to progress, and in issuing such a work Mr. Bell has entitled himself to the best thanks of every member of the trade."—*London Mining Journal.*

King's Notes on Steam.

Thirteenth Edition.

8vo. Cloth. $2.00.

LESSONS AND PRACTICAL NOTES ON STEAM, the Steam-Engine, Propellers, &c., &c., for Young Engineers, Students, and others. By the late W. R. KING, U. S. N. Revised by Chief-Engineer J. W. KING, U. S. Navy.

"This is one of the best, because eminently plain and practical treatises on the Steam Engine ever published.'—*Philadelphia Press.*

This is the thirteenth edition of a valuable work of the late W. H. King, U. S. N. It contains lessons and practical notes on Steam and the Steam Engine, Propellers, etc. It is calculated to be of great use to young marine engineers, students, and others. The text is illustrated and explained by numerous diagrams and representations of machinery.—*Boston Daily Advertiser.*

Text-book at the U. S. Naval Academy, Annapolis.

Burgh's Modern Marine Engineering.

One thick 4to vol. Cloth. $25.00. Half morocco. $30.00.

MODERN MARINE ENGINEERING, applied to Paddle and Screw Propulsion. Consisting of 36 Colored Plates, 259 Practical Wood-cut Illustrations, and 403 pages of Descriptive Matter, the whole being an exposition of the present practice of the following firms: Messrs. J. Penn & Sons; Messrs. Maudslay, Sons & Field; Messrs. James Watt & Co.; Messrs. J. & G. Rennie; Messrs. R. Napier & Sons; Messrs. J. & W. Dudgeon; Messrs. Ravenhill & Hodgson; Messrs. Humphreys & Tenant; Mr. J. T. Spencer, and Messrs. Forrester & Co. By N. P. Burgh, Engineer.

Principal Contents.—General Arrangements of Engines, 11 examples—General Arrangement of Boilers, 14 examples—General Arrangement of Superheaters, 11 examples—Details of Oscillating Paddle Engines, 34 examples—Condensers for Screw Engines, both Injection and Surface, 20 examples—Details of Screw Engines, 20 examples—Cylinders and Details of Screw Engines, 21 examples—Slide Valves and Details, 7 examples—Slide Valve, Link Motion, 7 examples—Expansion Valves and Gear, 10 examples—Details in General, 30 examples—Screw Propeller and Fittings, 13 examples - Engine and Boiler Fittings, 28 examples - In relation to the Principles of the Marine Engine and Boiler, 33 examples.

Notices of the Press.

"Every conceivable detail of the Marine Engine, under all its various forms, is profusely, and we must add, admirably illustrated by a multitude of engravings, selected from the best and most modern practice of the first Marine Engineers of the day. The chapter on Condensers is peculiarly valuable. In one word, there is no other work in existence which will bear a moment's comparison with it as an exponent of the skill, talent and practical experience to which is due the splendid reputation enjoyed by many British Marine Engineers."—*Engineer.*

"This very comprehensive work, which was issued in Monthly parts, has just been completed. It contains large and full drawings and copious descriptions of most of the best examples of Modern Marine Engines, and it is a complete theoretical and practical treatise on the subject of Marine Engineering."—*American Artisan.*

This is the only edition of the above work with the beautifully *colored* plates, and it is out of print in England.

Bourne's Treatise on the Steam Engine.

Ninth Edition.

Illustrated. 4to. Cloth. $15.00.

TREATISE ON THE STEAM ENGINE in its various applications to Mines, Mills, Steam Navigation, Railways, and Agriculture, with the theoretical investigations respecting the Motive Power of Heat and the proper Proportions of Steam Engines. Elaborate Tables of the right dimensions of every part, and Practical Instructions for the Manufacture and Management of every species of Engine in actual use. By JOHN BOURNE, being the ninth edition of "A Treatise on the Steam Engine," by the "Artisan Club." Illustrated by thirty-eight plates and five hundred and forty-six wood-cuts.

As Mr. Bourne's work has the great merit of avoiding unsound and immature views, it may safely be consulted by all who are really desirous of acquiring trustworthy information on the subject of which it treats. During the twenty-two years which have elapsed from the issue of the first edition, the improvements introduced in the construction of the steam engine have been both numerous and important, and of these Mr. Bourne has taken care to point out the more prominent, and to furnish the reader with such information as shall enable him readily to judge of their relative value. This edition has been thoroughly modernized, and made to accord with the opinions and practice of the more successful engineers of the present day. All that the book professes to give is given with ability and evident care. The scientific principles which are permanent are admirably explained, and reference is made to many of the more valuable of the recently introduced engines. To express an opinion of the value and utility of such a work as *The Artisan Club's Treatise on the Steam Engine*, which has passed through eight editions already, would be superfluous; but it may be safely stated that the work is worthy the attentive study of all either engaged in the manufacture of steam engines or interested in economizing the use of steam.—*Mining Journal.*

Isherwood's Engineering Precedents.

Two Vols. in One. 8vo. Cloth. $2.50.

ENGINEERING PRECEDENTS FOR STEAM MACHINERY. Arranged in the most practical and useful manner for Engineers. By B. F. ISHERWOOD, Civil Engineer, U. S. Navy. With illustrations.

Ward's Steam for the Million.

New and Revised Edition.

8vo. Cloth. $1.00.

STEAM FOR THE MILLION. A Popular Treatise on Steam and its Application to the Useful Arts, especially to Navigation. By J. H. Ward, Commander U. S. Navy. New and revised edition.

A most excellent work for the young engineer and general reader. Many facts relating to the management of the boiler and engine are set forth with a simplicity of language and perfection of detail that bring the subject home to the reader.—*American Engineer.*

Walker's Screw Propulsion.

8vo. Cloth. 75 cents.

NOTES ON SCREW PROPULSION, its Rise and History. By Capt. W. H. Walker, U. S. Navy.

Commander Walker's book contains an immense amount of concise practical data, and every item of information recorded fully proves that the various points bearing upon it have been well considered previously to expressing an opinion.—*London Mining Journal.*

Page's Earth's Crust.

18mo. Cloth. 75 cents.

THE EARTH'S CRUST: a Handy Outline of Geology. By David Page.

"Such a work as this was much wanted—a work giving in clear and intelligible outline the leading facts of the science, without amplification or irksome details. It is admirable in arrangement, and clear and easy, and, at the same time, forcible in style. It will lead, we hope, to the introduction of Geology into many schools that have neither time nor room for the study of large treatises."—*The Museum.*

Rogers' Geology of Pennsylvania.

3 Vols. 4to, with Portfolio of Maps. Cloth. $30.00.

THE GEOLOGY OF PENNSYLVANIA. A Government Survey. With a general view of the Geology of the United States, Essays on the Coal Formation and its Fossils, and a description of the Coal Fields of North America and Great Britain. By HENRY DARWIN ROGERS, Late State Geologist of Pennsylvania. Splendidly illustrated with Plates and Engravings in the Text.

It certainly should be in every public library throughout the country, and likewise in the possession of all students of Geology. After the final sale of these copies, the work will, of course, become more valuable.

The work for the last five years has been entirely out of the market, but a few copies that remained in the hands of Prof. Rogers, in Scotland, at the time of his death, are now offered to the public, at a price which is even below what it was originally sold for when first published.

Morfit on Pure Fertilizers.

With 28 Illustrative Plates. 8vo. Cloth. $20.00.

A PRACTICAL TREATISE ON PURE FERTILIZERS, and the Chemical Conversion of Rock Guanos, Marlstones, Coprolites, and the Crude Phosphates of Lime and Alumina Generally, into various Valuable Products. By CAMPBELL MORFIT, M.D., F.C.S.

Sweet's Report on Coal.

8vo. Cloth. $3.00.

SPECIAL REPORT ON COAL; showing its Distribution, Classification, and Cost delivered over different routes to various points in the State of New York, and the principal cities on the Atlantic Coast. By S. H. SWEET. With maps.

Colburn's Gas Works of London.

12mo. Boards. 60 cents.

GAS WORKS OF LONDON. By ZERAH COLBURN.

The Useful Metals and their Alloys; Scoffren, Truran, and others.

Fifth Edition.

8vo. Half calf. $3.75.

THE USEFUL METALS AND THEIR ALLOYS, including MINING VENTILATION, MINING JURISPRUDENCE AND METALLURGIC CHEMISTRY employed in the conversion of IRON, COPPER, TIN, ZINC, ANTIMONY, AND LEAD ORES, with their applications to THE INDUSTRIAL ARTS. By John Scoffren, William Truran, William Clay, Robert Oxland, William Fairbairn, W. C. Aitkin, and William Vose Pickett.

Collins' Useful Alloys.

18mo. Flexible. 75 cents.

THE PRIVATE BOOK OF USEFUL ALLOYS and Memoranda for Goldsmiths, Jewellers, etc. By James E. Collins

This little book is compiled from notes made by the Author from the papers of one of the largest and most eminent Manufacturing Goldsmiths and Jewellers in this country, and as the firm is now no longer in existence, and the Author is at present engaged in some other undertaking, he now offers to the public the benefit of his experience, and in so doing he begs to state that all the alloys, etc., given in these pages may be confidently relied on as being thoroughly practicable.

The Memoranda and Receipts throughout this book are also compiled from practice, and will no doubt be found useful to the practical jeweller. —*Shirley, July*, 1871.

Joynson's Metals Used in Construction.

12mo. Cloth. 75 cents.

THE METALS USED IN CONSTRUCTION: Iron, Steel, Bessemer Metal, etc., etc. By Francis Herbert Joynson. Illustrated.

"In the interests of practical science, we are bound to notice this work; and to those who wish further information, we should say, buy it; and the outlay, we honestly believe, will be considered well spent." —*Scientific Review.*

Holley's Ordnance and Armor.

493 Engravings. Half Roan, $10.00. Half Russia, $12.00.

A TREATISE ON ORDNANCE AND ARMOR—Embracing Descriptions, Discussions, and Professional Opinions concerning the MATERIAL, FABRICATION, Requirements, Capabilities, and Endurance of European and American Guns, for Naval, Sea Coast, and Iron-clad Warfare, and their RIFLING, PROJECTILES, and BREECH-LOADING; also, Results of Experiments against Armor, from Official Records, with an Appendix referring to Gun-Cotton, Hooped Guns, etc., etc. By ALEXANDER L. HOLLEY, B. P. 948 pages, 493 Engravings, and 147 Tables of Results, etc.

CONTENTS.

CHAPTER I.—Standard Guns and their Fabrication Described: Section 1. Hooped Guns; Section 2. Solid Wrought Iron Guns; Section 3. Solid Steel Guns; Section 4. Cast-Iron Guns. CHAPTER II.—The Requirements of Guns, Armor: Section 1. The Work to be done; Section 2. Heavy Shot at Low Velocities; Section 3. Small Shot at High Velocities; Section 4. The two Systems Combined; Section 5. Breaching Masonry. CHAPTER III.—The Strains and Structure of Guns: Section 1. Resistance to Elastic Pressure; Section 2. The Effects of Vibration; Section 3. The Effects of Heat. CHAPTER IV.—Cannon Metals and Processes of Fabrication: Section 1. Elasticity and Ductility; Section 2. Cast-Iron; Section 3. Wrought Iron; Section 4. Steel; Section 5. Bronze; Section 6. Other Alloys. CHAPTER V.—Rifling and Projectiles; Standard Forms and Practice Described; Early Experiments; The Centring System; The Compressing System; The Expansion System; Armor Punching Projectiles; Shells for Molten Metal; Competitive Trial of Rifled Guns, 1862; Duty of Rifled Guns: General Uses, Accuracy, Range, Velocity, Strain, Liability of Projectile to Injury; Firing Spherical Shot from Rifled Guns; Material for Armor-Punching Projectiles; Shape of Armor-Punching Projectiles; Capacity and Destructiveness of Shells; Elongated Shot from Smooth Bores; Conclusions; Velocity of Projectiles (Table). CHAPTER VI.—Breech-Loading Advantages and Defects of the System; Rapid Firing and Cooling Guns by Machinery; Standard Breech-Loaders Described. Part Second: Experiments against Armor; Account of Experiments from Official Records in Chronological Order. APPENDIX.—Report on the Application of Gun-Cotton to Warlike Purposes—British Association, 1863; Manufacture and Experiments in England; Guns Hooped with Initial Tension—History; How Guns Burst, by Wiard, Lyman's Accelerating Gun; Endurance of Parrott and Whitworth Guns at Charleston; Hooping old United States Cast-Iron Guns; Endurance and Accuracy of the Armstrong 600-pounder; Competitive Trials with 7-inch Guns.

Peirce's Analytic Mechanics.

4to. Cloth. $10.00.

SYSTEM OF ANALYTIC MECHANICS. Physical and Celestial Mechanics. By BENJAMIN PEIRCE, Perkins Professor of Astronomy and Mathematics in Harvard University, and Consulting Astronomer of the American Ephemeris and Nautical Almanac. Developed in four systems of Analytic Mechanics, Celestial Mechanics, Potential Physics, and Analytic Morphology.

"I have re-examined the memoirs of the great geometers, and have striven to consolidate their latest researches and their most exalted forms of thought into a consistent and uniform treatise. If I have hereby succeeded in opening to the students of my country a readier access to these choice jewels of intellect; if their brilliancy is not impaired in this attempt to reset them; if, in their own constellation, they illustrate each other, and concentrate a stronger light upon the names of their discoverers, and, still more, if any gem which I may have presumed to add is not wholly lustreless in the collection, I shall feel that my work has not been in vain."—*Extract from the Preface.*

Burt's Key to Solar Compass.

Second Edition.

Pocket Book Form. Tuck. $2.50.

KEY TO THE SOLAR COMPASS, and Surveyor's Companion; comprising all the Rules necessary for use in the field; also, Description of the Linear Surveys and Public Land System of the United States, Notes on the Barometer, Suggestions for an outfit for a Survey of four months, etc., etc., etc. By W. A. BURT, U. S. Deputy Surveyor. Second edition.

Chauvenet's Lunar Distances.

8vo. Cloth. $2.00.

NEW METHOD OF CORRECTING LUNAR DISTANCES, and Improved Method of Finding the Error and Rate of a Chronometer, by equal altitudes. By WM. CHAUVENET, LL.D., Chancellor of Washington University of St. Louis.

Jeffers' Nautical Surveying.

Illustrated with 9 Copperplates and 31 Wood-cut Illustrations. 8vo. Cloth. $5.00.

NAUTICAL SURVEYING. By WILLIAM N. JEFFERS, Captain U. S. Navy.

Many books have been written on each of the subjects treated of in the sixteen chapters of this work; and, to obtain a complete knowledge of geodetic surveying requires a profound study of the whole range of mathematical and physical sciences; but a year of preparation should render any intelligent officer competent to conduct a nautical survey.

CONTENTS.—Chapter I. Formulæ and Constants Useful in Surveying II. Distinctive Character of Surveys. III. Hydrographic Surveying under Sail; or, Running Survey. IV. Hydrographic Surveying of Boats; or, Harbor Survey. V. Tides—Definition of Tidal Phenomena—Tidal Observations. VI. Measurement of Bases—Appropriate and Direct. VII. Measurement of the Angles of Triangles—Azimuths—Astronomical Bearings. VIII. Corrections to be Applied to the Observed Angles. IX. Levelling—Difference of Level. X. Computation of the Sides of the Triangulation—The Three-point Problem. XI. Determination of the Geodetic Latitudes, Longitudes, and Azimuths, of Points of a Triangulation. XII. Summary of Subjects treated of in preceding Chapters—Examples of Computation by various Formulæ. XIII. Projection of Charts and Plans. XIV. Astronomical Determination of Latitude and Longitude. XV. Magnetic Observations. XVI. Deep Sea Soundings. XVII. Tables for Ascertaining Distances at Sea, and a full Index.

List of Plates.

Plate I. Diagram Illustrative of the Triangulation. II. Specimen Page of Field Book. III. Running Survey of a Coast. IV. Example of a Running Survey from Belcher. V. Flying Survey of an Island. VI. Survey of a Shoal. VII. Boat Survey of a River. VIII. Three-Point Problem. IX. Triangulation.

Coffin's Navigation.

Fifth Edition.

12mo. Cloth. $3.50.

NAVIGATION AND NAUTICAL ASTRONOMY. Prepared for the use of the U. S. Naval Academy. By J. H. C. COFFIN, Prof. of Astronomy, Navigation and Surveying, with 52 woodcut illustrations.

Clark's Theoretical Navigation.

8vo. Cloth. $3.00.

THEORETICAL NAVIGATION AND NAUTICAL ASTRONOMY. By LEWIS CLARK, Lieut.-Commander, U. S. Navy. Illustrated with 41 Wood-cuts, including the Vernier.

Prepared for Use at the U. S. Naval Academy.

The Plane Table.

Illustrated. 8vo. Cloth. $2.00.

ITS USES IN TOPOGRAPHICAL SURVEYING. From the Papers of the U. S. Coast Survey.

This work gives a description of the Plane Table employed at the U. S. Coast Survey Office, and the manner of using it.

Pook on Shipbuilding.

8vo. Cloth. $5.00.

METHOD OF COMPARING THE LINES AND DRAUGHTING VESSELS PROPELLED BY SAIL OR STEAM, including a Chapter on Laying off on the Mould-Loft Floor. By SAMUEL M. POOK, Naval Constructor. 1 vol., 8vo. With illustrations. Cloth. $5.00.

Brunnow's Spherical Astronomy.

8vo. Cloth. $6.50.

SPHERICAL ASTRONOMY. By F. BRUNNOW, Ph. Dr. Translated by the Author from the Second German edition.

Van Buren's Formulas.

8vo. Cloth. $2.00.

INVESTIGATIONS OF FORMULAS, for the Strength of the Iron Parts of Steam Machinery. By J. D. VAN BUREN, JR., C. E. Illustrated.

This is an analytical discussion of the formulæ employed by mechanical engineers in determining the rupturing or crippling pressure in the different parts of a machine. The formulæ are founded upon the principle, that the different parts of a machine should be equally strong, and are developed in reference to the ultimate strength of the material in order to leave the choice of a factor of safety to the judgment of the designer.—*Silliman's Journal.*

Joynson on Machine Gearing.

8vo. Cloth. $2.00.

THE MECHANIC'S AND STUDENT'S GUIDE in the Designing and Construction of General Machine Gearing, as Eccentrics, Screws, Toothed Wheels, etc., and the Drawing of Rectilineal and Curved Surfaces; with Practical Rules and Details. Edited by FRANCIS HERBERT JOYNSON. Illustrated with 18 folded plates.

"The aim of this work is to be a guide to mechanics in the designing and construction of general machine-gearing. This design it well fulfils, being plainly and sensibly written, and profusely illustrated."—*Sunday Times.*

Barnard's Report, Paris Exposition, 1867.

Illustrated. 8vo. Cloth. $5.00.

REPORT ON MACHINERY AND PROCESSES ON THE INDUSTRIAL ARTS AND APPARATUS OF THE EXACT SCIENCES. By F. A. P. BARNARD, LL.D.—Paris Universal Exposition, 1867.

"We have in this volume the results of Dr. Barnard's study of the Paris Exposition of 1867, in the form of an official Report of the Government. It is the most exhaustive treatise upon modern inventions that has appeared since the Universal Exhibition of 1851, and we doubt if anything equal to it has appeared this century."—*Journal Applied Chemistry.*

Engineering Facts and Figures.

18mo. Cloth. $2.50 per Volume.

AN ANNUAL REGISTER OF PROGRESS IN MECHANICAL ENGINEERING AND CONSTRUCTION, for the Years 1863–64–65–66–67–68. Fully illustrated. 6 volumes.

Each volume sold separately.

Beckwith's Pottery.

8vo. Paper. 60 cents.

OBSERVATIONS ON THE MATERIALS and Manufacture of Terra-Cotta, Stone-Ware, Fire-Brick, Porcelain and Encaustic Tiles, with Remarks on the Products exhibited at the London International Exhibition, 1871. By ARTHUR BECKWITH, Civil Engineer.

"Everything is noticed in this book which comes under the head of Pottery, from fine porcelain to ordinary brick, and aside from the interest which all take in such manufactures, the work will be of considerable value to followers of the ceramic art."—*Evening Mail.*

Dodd's Dictionary of Manufactures, etc.

12mo. Cloth. $2.00.

DICTIONARY OF MANUFACTURES, MINING, MACHINERY, AND THE INDUSTRIAL ARTS. By GEORGE DODD.

This work, a small book on a great subject, treats, in alphabetical arrangement, of those numerous matters which come generally within the range of manufactures and the productive arts. The raw materials—animal, vegetable, and mineral—whence the manufactured products are derived, are succinctly noticed in connection with the processes which they undergo, but not as subjects of natural history. The operations of the Mine and the Mill, the Foundry and the Forge, the Factory and the Workshop, are passed under review. The principal machines and engines, tools and apparatus, concerned in manufacturing processes, are briefly described. The scale on which our chief branches of national industry are conducted, in regard to values and quantities, is indicated in various ways.

Stuart's Civil and Military Engineering of America.

8vo. Illustrated. Cloth. $5.00.

THE CIVIL AND MILITARY ENGINEERS OF AMERICA. By General Charles B. Stuart, Author of "Naval Dry Docks of the United States," etc., etc. Embellished with nine finely executed portraits on steel of eminent engineers, and illustrated by engravings of some of the most important and original works constructed in America.

Containing sketches of the Life and Works of Major Andrew Ellicott, James Geddes (with Portrait), Benjamin Wright (with Portrait), Canvass White (with Portrait), David Stanhope Bates, Nathan S. Roberts, Gridley Bryant (with Portrait), General Joseph G. Swift, Jesse L. Williams (with Portrait), Colonel William McRee, Samuel H. Kneass, Captain John Childe with Portrait), Frederick Harbach, Major David Bates Douglas (with Portrait), Jonathan Knight, Benjamin H. Latrobe (with Portrait), Colonel Charles Ellet, Jr. (with Portrait), Samuel Forrer, William Stuart Watson, John A. Roebling.

Alexander's Dictionary of Weights and Measures.

8vo. Cloth. $3.50.

UNIVERSAL DICTIONARY OF WEIGHTS AND MEASURES, Ancient and Modern, reduced to the standards of the United States of America. By J. H. Alexander. New edition. 1 vol.

"As a standard work of reference, this book should be in every library; it is one which we have long wanted, and it will save much trouble and research."—*Scientific American.*

Gouge on Ventilation.

Third Edition Enlarged.

8vo. Cloth. $2.00.

NEW SYSTEM OF VENTILATION, which has been thoroughly tested under the patronage of many distinguished persons. By Henry A. Gouge, with many illustrations.

Saeltzer's Acoustics.

12mo. Cloth. $2.00.

TREATISE ON ACOUSTICS in Connection with Ventilation. With a new theory based on an important discovery, of facilitating clear and intelligible sound in any building. By ALEXANDER SAELTZER.

"A practical and very sound treatise on a subject of great importance to architects, and one to which there has hitherto been entirly too little attention paid. The author's theory is, that, by bestowing proper care upon the point of Acoustics, the requisite ventilation will be obtained, and *vice versa.*—*Brooklyn Union.*

Myer's Manual of Signals.

New Edition. Enlarged.

12mo. 48 Plates full Roan. $5.00.

MANUAL OF SIGNALS, for the Use of Signal Officers in the Field, and for Military and Naval Students, Military Schools, etc. A new edition, enlarged and illustrated. By Brig.-Gen. ALBERT J. MYER, Chief Signal Officer of the Army, Colonel of the Signal Corps during the War of the Rebellion.

Larrabee's Secret Letter and Telegraph Code.

18mo. Cloth. $1.00.

CIPHER AND SECRET LETTER AND TELEGRAPHIC CODE, with Hogg's Improvements. The most perfect secret Code ever invented or discovered. Impossible to read without the Key. Invaluable for Secret, Military, Naval, and Diplomatic Service, as well as for Brokers, Bankers, and Merchants. By C. S. LARRABEE, the original inventor of the scheme.

Hunt's Designs for Central Park Gateways.

4to. Cloth. $5.00.

DESIGNS FOR THE GATEWAYS OF THE SOUTHERN ENTRANCES TO THE CENTRAL PARK. By RICHARD M. HUNT. With a description of the designs.

Pickert and Metcalf's Art of Graining.

1 vol. 4to. Cloth. $10.00.

THE ART OF GRAINING. How Acquired and How Produced, with description of colors and their application. By CHARLES PICKERT and ABRAHAM METCALF. Beautifully illustrated with 42 tinted plates of the various woods used in interior finishing. Tinted paper.

The authors present here the result of long experience in the practice of this decorative art, and feel confident that they hereby offer to their brother artisans a reliable guide to improvement in the practice of graining.

Portrait Gallery of the War.

60 fine Portraits on Steel. Royal 8vo. Cloth. $6.00.

PORTRAIT GALLERY OF THE WAR, CIVIL, MILITARY AND NAVAL. A Biographical Record. Edited by FRANK MOORE.

One Law in Nature.

12mo. Cloth. $1.50.

ONE LAW IN NATURE. By Capt. H. M. LAZELLE, U. S. A. A New Corpuscular Theory, comprehending Unity of Force, Identity of Matter, and its Multiple Atom Constitution, applied to the Physical Affections or Modes of Energy.

Ernst's Manual of Military Engineering.

193 Wood Cuts and 3 Lithographed Plates. 12mo. Cloth. $5.00.

A MANUAL OF PRACTICAL MILITARY ENGINEERING. Prepared for the use of the Cadets of the U. S. Military Academy, and for Engineer Troops. By Capt. O. H. ERNST, Corps of Engineers, Instructor in Practical Military Engineering, U. S. Military Academy.

Church's Metallurgical Journey.

24 Illustrations. 8vo. Cloth. $2.00.

NOTES OF A METALLURGICAL JOURNEY IN EUROPE. By JOHN A. CHURCH, Engineer of Mines.

Blake's Precious Metals.

8vo. Cloth. $2.00.

REPORT UPON THE PRECIOUS METALS: Being Statistical Notices of the principal Gold and Silver producing regions of the World. Represented at the Paris Universal Exposition. By WILLIAM P. BLAKE, Commissioner from the State of California.

Clevenger's Surveying.

Illustrated Pocket Form. Morocco Gilt. $2.50.

A TREATISE ON THE METHOD OF GOVERNMENT SURVEYING, as prescribed by the United States Congress. and Commissioner of the General Land Office. With complete Mathematical, Astronomical and Practical Instructions, for the use of the United States Surveyors in the Field, and Students who contemplate engaging in the business of Public Land Surveying. By S. R. CLEVENGER, U. S. Deputy Surveyor.

"The reputation of the author as a surveyor guarantees an exhaustive treatise on this subject."—*Dakota Register.*

"Surveyors have long needed a text-book of this description.—*The Press.*

Bow on Bracing.

156 Illustrations on Stone. 8vo. Cloth. $1.50.

A TREATISE ON BRACING, with its application to Bridges and other Structures of Wood or Iron. By ROBERT HENRY BOW, C. E.

Howard's Earthwork Mensuration.

8vo. Illustrated. Cloth. $1.50.

EARTHWORK MENSURATION ON THE BASIS OF THE PRISMOIDAL FORMULÆ. Containing simple and labor-saving method of obtaining Prismoidal Contents directly from End Areas. Illustrated by Examples, and accompanied by Plain Rules for practical uses. By CONWAY R. HOWARD, Civil Engineer, Richmond, Va.

McAlpine's Modern Engineering.

Second Edition. 8vo. Cloth. $1.50.

MODERN ENGINEERING. A Lecture delivered at the American Institute in New York. By WILLIAM J. MCALPINE.

Mowbray's Tri-Nitro-Glycerine.

8vo. Cloth. Illustrated. $3.00.

TRI-NITRO-GLYCERINE, as applied in the Hoosac Tunnel, and to Submarine Blasting, Torpedoes, Quarrying, etc. Being the result of six years' observation and practice during the manufacture of five hundred thousand pounds of this explosive, Mica Blasting Powder, Dynamites; with an account of the various Systems of Blasting by Electricity, Priming Compounds, Explosives, etc., etc. By GEORGE M. MOWBRAY, Operative Chemist, with thirteen illustrations, tables, and appendix. Third Edition. Re-written.

Wanklyn's Milk Analysis.

12mo. Cloth. $1.00.

MILK ANALYSIS. A Practical Treatise on the Examination of Milk, and its Derivatives, Cream, Butter and Cheese. By J. ALFRED WANKLYN, M. R. C. S.

Toner's Dictionary of Elevations.

8vo. Paper, $3.00. Cloth, $3.75.

DICTIONARY OF ELEVATIONS AND CLIMATIC REGISTER OF THE UNITED STATES. Containing, in addition to Elevations, the Latitude, Mean Annual Temperature, and the total Annual Rain Fall of many localities; with a brief Introduction on the Orographic and Physical Peculiarities of North America. By J. M. TONER, M. D.

Adams. Sewers and Drains.

(*In Press.*)

SEWERS AND DRAINS FOR POPULOUS DISTRICTS. Embracing Rules and Formulas for the dimensions of Sanitary Engineers. By JULIUS W. ADAMS, Chief Engineer of the Board of City Works, Brooklyn.

Prescott's Proximate Organic Analysis.

12mo. Cloth. $1.75.

OUTLINES OF PROXIMATE ORGANIC ANALYSIS for the Identification, Separation, and Quantitative Determination of the more commonly occurring Organic Compounds. By ALBERT B. PRESCOTT, Professor of Organic and Applied Chemistry in the University of Michigan.

Prescott's Alcoholic Liquors.

12mo. Cloth. $1.50.

CHEMICAL EXAMINATION OF ALCOHOLIC LIQUORS. A Manual of the Constituents of the Distilled Spirits and Fermented Liquors of Commerce, and their Qualitative and Quantitative Determinations. By ALBERT B. PRESCOTT, Professor of Organic and Applied Chemistry in the University of Michigan.

Greene's Bridge Trusses.

8vo. Illustrated. Cloth. $2.00.

GRAPHICAL METHOD FOR THE ANALYSIS OF BRIDGE TRUSSES, extended to Continuous Girders and Draw Spans. By CHARLES E. GREENE, A.M., Professor of Civil Engineering, University of Michigan. Illustrated by three folding plates.

Butler's Projectiles and Rifled Cannon.

4to. 32 Plates. Cloth. In press.

PROJECTILES AND RIFLED CANNON. A Critical Discussion of the Principal Systems of Rifling and Projectiles, with Practical Suggestions for their Improvement, as embraced in a Report to the Chief of Ordnance, U.S.A. By Capt. JOHN S. BUTLER, Ordnance Corps, U.S.A.

Van Nostrand's Science Series.

It is the intention of the Publisher of this Series to issue them at intervals of about a month. They will be put up in a uniform, neat and attractive form, 18mo, fancy boards. The subjects will be of an eminently scientific character, and embrace as wide a range of topics as possible, all of the highest character.

Price, 50 Cents Each.

1.

CHIMNEYS FOR FURNACES, FIRE-PLACES, AND STEAM BOILERS. By R. Armstrong, C. E.

2.

STEAM BOILER EXPLOSIONS. By Zerah Colburn.

3.

PRACTICAL DESIGNING OF RETAINING WALLS By Arthur Jacob, A. B. With Illustrations.

4.

PROPORTIONS OF PINS USED IN BRIDGES. By Charles E. Bender, C. E. With Illustrations.

5.

VENTILATION OF BUILDINGS. By W. F. Butler. With Illustrations.

6.

ON THE DESIGNING AND CONSTRUCTION OF STORAGE RESERVOIRS. By Arthur Jacob. With Illustrations.

7.

SURCHARGED AND DIFFERENT FORMS OF RETAINING WALLS. By James S. Tate, C. E.

8.

A TREATISE ON THE COMPOUND ENGINE. By John Turnbull. With Illustrations.

9.

FUEL. By C. W. Siemens to which is appended the Value of Artificial Fuels as compared with Coal. By J. Wormald, C. E.

*** Other works in preparation.

10.

COMPOUND ENGINES. Translated from the French of A. MALLET. Illustrated.

11.

THEORY OF ARCHES. By Prof. W. ALLAN, of the Washington and Lee College. Illustrated.

12.

A PRACTICAL THEORY OF VOUSSOIR ARCHES. By WILLIAM CAIN, C.E. Illustrated.

13.

A PRACTICAL TREATISE ON THE GASES MET WITH IN COAL-MINES. By the late J. J. ATKINSON, Government Inspector of Mines for the County of Durham, England.

14.

FRICTION OF AIR IN MINES. By J. J. ATKINSON, Author of "A Practical Treatise on the Gases met with in Coal-Mines."

15.

SKEW ARCHES. By Prof. E. W. HYDE, C.E. Illustrated with numerous engravings and three folded plates.

SILVER MINING REGIONS OF COLORADO, with some account of the different Processes now being introduced for working the Gold Ores of that Territory. By J. P. WHITNEY. 12mo. Paper. 25 cents.

COLORADO: SCHEDULE OF ORES contributed by sundry persons to the Paris Universal Exposition of 1867, with some information about the Region and its Resources. By J. P. WHITNEY, Commissioner from the Territory. 8vo. Paper, with Maps. 25 cents.

THE SILVER DISTRICTS OF NEVADA. With Map. 8vo. Paper. 35 cents.

ARIZONA: ITS RESOURCES AND PROSPECTS. By Hon. R. C. McCORMICK, Secretary of the Territory. With Map. 8vo. Paper. 25 cents.

MONTANA AS IT IS. Being a general description of its Resources, both Mineral and Agricultural; including a complete description of the face of the country, its climate, etc. Illustrated with a Map of the Territory, showing the different Roads and the location of the different Mining Districts. To which is appended a complete Dictionary of THE SNAKE LANGUAGE, and also of the famous Chinnook Jargon, with numerous critical and explanatory Notes. By GRANVILLE STUART. 8vo. Paper. $2.00.

RAILWAY GAUGES. A Review of the Theory of Narrow Gauges as applied to Main Trunk Lines of Railway. By SILAS SEYMOUR, Genl. Consulting Engineer. 8vo. Paper. 50 cents.

REPORT made to the President and Executive Board of the Texas Pacific Railroad. By Gen. G. P. BUELL, Chief Engineer. 8vo. Paper. 75 cents.

www.ingramcontent.com/pod-product-compliance
Lightning Source LLC
LaVergne TN
LVHW021405110826
845150LV00007B/1794

* 9 7 8 1 4 2 5 5 1 2 2 7 9 *